OUR SOUTHERN LANDSMAN

Books by Harry Golden

Our Southern

HARRY GOLDEN
author of ONLY IN AMERICA

Landsman

G. P. PUTNAM'S SONS, NEW YORK

Cop. 1

COPYRIGHT © 1974 BY HARRY GOLDEN

SBN: 399-11130-1
Library of Congress Catalog Card Number: 72-97293

"The Savannah Accession" was first published in the Savannah *News-Press*, April 16, 1972, under the title of "Savannah's First Jews." "The First Kennedy" appeared in the Baltimore *Sun Magazine*, March 19, 1972.

PRINTED IN THE UNITED STATES OF AMERICA

*Dedicated to the South, where I've met
some of the kindest people in the world*

I am grateful to two of my sons, Richard Goldhurst, of Westport, Connecticut, who did the research in Savannah, Richmond, and Baltimore, and my youngest son, Professor William Goldhurst, the University of Florida at Gainesville, Florida, for his help in researching and editing the manuscript.

Special thanks are also given to the American Jewish Archives on the Cincinnati Campus of the Hebrew Union College, Jewish Institute of Religion, for the right granted to the author and publisher to reproduce the illustrations contained in this volume.

Contents

11

Contents

INTRODUCTION

THERE MUST BE a moment in the life of every President when he realizes he has nominated his last Supreme Court Justice.

Arthur Goldberg not long ago told me about his nomination when Felix Frankfurter stepped down. President Kennedy told him he was sending his name up. "But we'll miss you around here," said the President.

Goldberg, who was serving as Secretary of Labor, suggested Kennedy send his name up the next time.

"There may not be a next time," Kennedy sighed.

Each time I finish a book I wonder if it will be the last one I send up.

However, sending up the names of nominees is a duty a President may not shirk—*vide* Richard Nixon. And the next book is always the dearest and the best to a writer.

What inspired this thinking was the comment of a wise and comic friend. He said when I died, I would probably go to the Lower East Side.

Personally, I said, I do not want to go to the Lower East Side. If I have my druthers, I want to go to the Berkeley-Carteret Hotel on the Boardwalk in Atlantic City *circa*

1925, which is where I spent my honeymoon. Atlantic City was something in those days.

And anyone else who thinks I can go only to the Lower East Side ought to be reminded that I have written more about the South than I have about any other place. Or any other states of mind.

Mr. Kennedy and the Negroes, A Little Girl Is Dead, and *The Right Time* deal directly with the South. And so does this book, which describes the story of Jews in the South. It is a congenial subject, made congenial because I understand a basic truth about the Jews who live in the United States. That basic truth is that there is a difference between the Jews who live in New York City and the Jews who do not. The Jews in New York City have a hard time in realizing that not only are there places where you cannot buy pastrami in the United States, but there are places which haven't even heard of rye bread.

I am seventy years old as I write this. On the whole, it isn't fun except for the opportunity to learn from your mistakes.

There are a variety of ways in which we learn. For instance, I was the editor of a small monthly journal who hired a prisoner on the work release system. If more editors hired prisoners on the work release system, there would be no more work release system.

H. G.

OUR SOUTHERN LANDSMAN

Our Southern Landsman

IT IS POSSIBLE to write a history of the Jews of New York City without once mentioning the Erie Canal which opened in 1825. The Erie Canal determined the preeminence of New York as the great American port. But the Jews were neither shippers nor farmers and manufacturers in the Midwest.

It is possible to write a history of the Jews of Cleveland without once mentioning the terms by which Connecticut saved for itself a 300,000-acre tract on the Cuyahoga River known as the Western Reserve. There were no Jews in Ohio when Moses Cleaveland staked out Cleveland in 1796 for the Connecticut Land Company.

It is possible to write about the Jews of California without once having to describe the campaign of General John Frémont in 1846 which helped realize America's "Manifest Destiny." There were almost no Norteamericanos in California until the Swiss John Sutter heard someone had discovered gold in his creek.

But it is impossible to write a history of the Jews of the South without re-creating the history of the South itself.

Consider the reasons.

There were always Jews in the South, but there was always a paucity of them.

As a matter of fact, there were only 3,000 Jews in all the thirteen colonies in 1776. They did not constitute 1 percent of the population of North America, which was then 4,000,000. Of more than 3,000 houses of worship at the beginning of the Revolutionary War, only 5 were Jewish. Two of these congregations were in the South—Mikvah Israel in Savannah and Beth Elohim in Charleston, South Carolina. It is well to remember that there were exactly 68 Jews in Charleston in 1776, and there couldn't have been 40 in all Georgia.

Of the 68 Jews in Charleston, some went to fight for the Continental Army, some had families and could not afford to fight, and some cooperated with the British when they invested the city in 1779–80. We know there were Jewish Patriots because their names were carried on the rolls of the Carolina militia. We know there were Jewish Tories because South Carolina amerced their property with the Confiscation Act of 1783.

In Savannah, Mordechai Sheftall became the commissary general for the Continental Army and was captured by the British. His half brother, Levi, stayed home and made money by a variety of enterprises which ranged from skinning deer to keeping store.

For a century at least, the history of the Jews of the South is a series of anecdotes about men who happened to be Jewish and were caught up in the events history deposited at their doorstep.

The 3,000 Colonial Jews of 1776 had become 250,000 by 1870. German Jews had begun emigrating to America at the end of the Napoleonic Wars. After the abortive Revolution of 1848, they came to America by the shipload.

The pioneers among them pushed out from New York to Hartford and Cincinnati and St. Louis, but only a small number went South.

The South was an agrarian economy. The residency of Jews in the United States has been marked by their preference for the industrial cities. Seventy percent of all the Jews in America live in sixteen cities, only one of which, Miami, is in the South and only two of which, Baltimore and St. Louis, have any Southern coloration. There are 6,200,000 Jews in the United States. Between Miami and Dallas, Dallas and Baltimore there are 540,000.

After the Civil War, of course, the South had no economy. It was broken in two. Few immigrants of any nationality ventured into it. The Jews of the South, in fact, began emigrating north after 1865 because there was no livelihood for them in the bankrupted Southern cities.

Thus, because of the scarcity of their numbers, there was never a Jewish complement in the South. A complement of Jews, indeed a large complement, transformed the needle trades of New York into the garment industry. Another complement of Jews, indeed a minuscule complement, established the movie industry in California. Another complement founded Union Theological Seminary in Cincinnati. And a complement of Jewish merchants and publishers and bankers became the "Our Crowd" of which Stephen Birmingham has written so tellingly.

Here and there a Jew founded a school in the South, but it was not a Jewish school. There is a Levy's in Savannah and a Feibelman's in New Orleans, but there was never an "Our Crowd" in the South, except perhaps the textile Cones of Greensboro, North Carolina. Isaiah Wolf Hellman, who came to Los Angeles in 1859, started the multibillion-dollar Farmers and Merchants Bank by offering prospectors current rates for the gold dust and holding this money on deposit. Kaspare Cohn and Harris Newmark became Hellman's banking competitors by lending money to Basque shepherds in the San Gabriel Mountains. The Jewish-controlled International Ladies Garment Workers Union has become a banking institution by lending money to employers. But the nature of the South precluded credit as an enterprise. There were few of the traditional professions for the Jews in the South.

It is also true that the Jews in America were not *organized as Jews* until the advent of the East European immigrants which began in 1880. That is to say that though Jews had founded synagogues and community centers, they had not joined together to realize certain philanthropic and political interests.

But the influx of poor East European immigrant Jews damaged the advantageous social position of the now-assimilated German Jews. As Oscar Handlin puts it in *Adventure in Freedom*, "Charity, traditionally a virtue of Jews, became a categorical imperative."

The rich Jews began to found hospitals and community centers and Educational Alliances to facilitate the assimilation of these immigrants. To do this quickly and efficiently, the German Jews federated their energies and their monies. Thus was the Jewish entity born.

So in many respects, before the 1880's the history of the Jews in the North and the Midwest and Far West is also discursive—based on the derring-do or good luck of individuals.

This is not to say that the Jews of the South are without a history. The lynching of Leo Frank in Georgia in 1915 is certainly part of that history, but what happened to Leo

Frank did not happen to every Jew, and what happened to the Jews of Atlanta in 1915 did not keep happening, though indeed racists tried to keep it happening. Instead, there were a variety of Jews, and a variety of things happened to them.

I. D. Blumenthal, my first employer in Charlotte, came south after World War I. I. D. was out for a ride in his tin lizzie in the 1920's when the afternoon's joy was interrupted by a leaking radiator. I. D. pulled over to a roadstand station which had a gas pump among the collard greens, okra, and turnips. The attendant, whose pants were supported by the strand of one suspender, said he could fix the radiator "right smart quick," and from a kerosene pitcher he poured a solution into a handful of sawdust which he stuffed down the funnel of the radiator. Lo and behold, the leak was plugged.

The ever-curious I. D. asked the man about the solution's elements. How had he come to devise such a clever compound? The fellow told I. D. the composition of the solution and added that he had learned the trick when he was in the motor pool of Camp Lucky Strike in France— except in the Army they used dried horse shit instead of sawdust.

To show his gratitude, I. D. bought a basket of turnips and drove off. But I. D. was now a man consumed by a vision, a flaming vision like that which consumed Jeanne d'Arc at Orléans or Washington at Valley Forge. Everyone in the United States was going to have a car, and every car was going to have a radiator. I. D. was on his way to marketing the first radiator sealant. Made a good thing of it, too. Even figured how to get rid of the sawdust.

The history of the Jews in the South is a story told

23

geographically rather than psychologically, and it centers on men and women and their motivations, rather than causes and progress, for its narrative.

There were Jews who came South to hide their identities and others who fought tirelessly for their rights. Jews gave their lives for the Confederacy, and one, at least, not only gave all his own money but all of other people's money, too. He was Benjamin Mordechai of Charleston, who contributed $10,000 to the Cause as soon as South Carolina seceded. His faith was of such proportions he invested the rest of his fortune in Confederate bonds. His enthusiasm kept surging, however, and since he was the trustee for a large estate, he sank that money into the Cause as well.

After the war, the beneficiary filed suit against the patriotic Mordechai and won. The judge offered the opinion that the trustee had no business "risking to the chances of the whirlpool" money entrusted to his care. A lot of good it did the beneficiary.

The Crypto Jews and the First Jewish Governor

THE FIRST JEW in Virginia was probably Dr. John de Sequeyra, also known as Siccari, who kept his identity a secret. A Marrano, a convert who accepted conversion to escape the inquisitorial pyre, De Sequeyra was born in London in 1712 and, after being graduated as a physician from the University of Leiden in Holland, came to Williamsburg in 1745.

He lived in a house so perfectly Colonial it didn't need restoration when Williamsburg went public, as it were.

Dr. de Sequeyra did not worship openly if he worshiped

at all, nor did he openly engage in theological disputations. But he enjoyed a wide and influential circle of friends and on several occasions attended Colonel Washington's step-daughter Patsy Custis.

De Sequeyra played a crucial role in American gastronomical history according to no less an authority than Thomas Jefferson. De Sequeyra introduced the tomato as a vegetable to the dining table. He believed a man who ate enough tomatoes would never die. Since he lived to the ripe old age of eighty-three, he probably thought to the last that he had hit upon something.

Another crypto Jew became the sixth governor of Georgia, the first Jew in America to become a governor. He was David Emmanuel, born in Pennsylvania in 1744. He was also one of the first Americans to be a returning POW.

Emmanuel fought in Georgia during the Revolutionary War and was taken prisoner by the British with two of his fellow officers, Lewis and Davis, after the Battle of McBean's Peak in Burke County. Captain Bradley, their British captor, put the three to menial tasks, and after they had built a bonfire for the bivouac, Bradley ordered them to undress in front of it. The three Americans thought this was to inhibit any attempt to escape, but Bradley wanted to distribute their clothes to some mulattoes who bummed along with his company.

When the Americans had handed over their clothes, Bradley ordered three British regulars to shoot them. Lewis and Davis fell, but Emmanuel's executioner missed. Emmanuel leaped through the fire, dodged between the horses, and ran to the swamp, where he spent terror-ridden hours listening to the curses of his pursuers.

After the war, Emmanuel represented Burke County in the legislature and in 1797 became president of the Senate.

He was sworn in as governor on March 3, 1801, and died in 1808. Emmanuel's Jewishness seems to have been covert by carelessness rather than design. After his death, an admiring contemporary remarked that the governor's two daughters had married Christian gentlemen, there being no Jews in Waynesboro.

Nor were the crypto Jews only colonial Jews. David Ovens, né Ovinsky, stepped off a train in Charlotte one afternoon in 1902 and put an end to his Jewishness. He was a restless young man who had come to North Carolina because it was as far away as he could afford from the cold in Montreal.

Within a week he landed a job with a wholesale grocer named J. B. Ivey. Ivey was a shrewd businessman, and Ovens had an inexhaustible supply of merchandising ideas.

A year later Ivey founded his department store (which in 1973 had more than twenty branches in four Southern states), and Ovens went with him as a junior and later equal partner. J. B. and Ovens amassed a respectable fortune with which they did good deeds for the church. Ovens built filigreed iron fences around every Presbyterian church in North Carolina. He was an unending source of fence money, and when Ovens ran out of Presbyterians, he built fences for the Episcopalians. J. B. refused to sell gaming devices of any description in his stores, and on Sundays he pulled large green blinds over the windows lest the sight of commerce desecrate the Lord's Day.

Ovens particularly interested me because he was the hero of Burke Davis' novel *Whisper My Name*. Burke was the first Gentile who became my friend in the South, the first Gentile, in fact, who invited me into his home. Burke was a newspaperman on the Charlotte *News*. He had not only deep liberal convictions but deep liberal convictions on the race issue, a rare bird in the South of 1943.

Whisper My Name was Burke's first book, and the Jew of the novel gets off the train at Charlotte, looks in the faces of passing Christians, and says to himself, "That's what I want to be, that's how I want to look."

As he worked away, Burke showed me the book, and I occasionally advised him about the actions of a Jew new to a Southern town. *Whisper My Name* didn't make Burke's reputation; *Gray Fox*, a biography of Robert E. Lee, did. But I think a canny publisher would realize money by reissuing Burke's novel. Burke is now historian in residence at Williamsburg.

I heard the whispers about Ovens as soon as I got to Charlotte. I met him only once. He was a short man with white hair and rimless spectacles and he was the personification of Southern dignity. I was soliciting for the Joint Distribution Committee, the forerunner of the UJA, and Ovens turned me down. But he turned me down politely.

Some years after his death, the Charlotte City Council voted to name the new municipal auditorium in his honor. One of the newspapers took the City Council to task. The editorial argued the auditorium should be known as the Charlotte Auditorium instead of the Ovens Auditorium. The duty of the City Council, the editor went on, was not to celebrate the past but to promote the future. Charlotte was the future. But the City Council won.

Not all these crypto Jews wanted to disguise their identity. Some of them lost it because they joined other tribes as it were. A case in point, perhaps the most romantic Jew ever to come to the South, was dark-eyed Abram Mordechai, a Jew born in Pennsylvania in 1755, who founded the city of Montgomery, Alabama.

A butcher, Abram Mordechai served three years in the ranks of the Continental Army and decided to better himself by moving South. In 1783, Mordechai settled among the Cusewata Indians who lived at Buzzard's Roost on the Flint River in Georgia. He lived like an Indian and married one, although an Indian agent once described his wife as one "darkened by the blood of Ham."

Abram Mordechai traded with the Corvalla Indians in the western part of the state. He dealt in skins, fur, pinkroot, and other medicinal bark which he transported by packhorse to Augusta, Pensacola, and Mobile. He traveled as far as Polecat Springs, Alabama, where he asked Colonel Hawkins, the Indian agent, about the prospects of opening a store and cotton gin, thereby to instruct Indians in the arts of civilization. Hawkins suggested Mordechai establish a gin and a store on the bluffs just below the junction of the Coosa and Tallapoosa rivers, the site of present-day Montgomery.

Peace and industry were not concomitants of frontier life. One afternoon in 1805, Mordechai was summoned from his store by Towerculla, chief of the Creek Nation. The chief was accompanied by sixteen braves all carrying the ceremonial war poles of stout hickory. The Indians laid on. Finally, Towerculla knelt beside the bleeding, near-dead man and with his knife cut off Mordechai's left ear. The Indians burned down Mordechai's store and chopped up his new boat which cost $400. Then they left him to the care of his wife.

It was several months before Mordechai could walk again, and for the rest of his life his body bore the welts raised by the merciless beating. He said two of his horses which strayed into Towerculla's cornfields provoked the attack.

Towerculla had a different explanation. He said that the next time Mordechai made ficky-fac with a chief's "squaw" he would lose the other ear.

Mordechai, dispossessed and dispirited, returned to Georgia. He fought in the battles of Autussi and Calabee in 1813. In 1814 Mordechai returned to the Creek and took up the building of Montgomery.

When a certain Rabbi A. J. Messing from Philadelphia asked Abram Mordechai, who was then ninety, why he had chosen to spend his life with the Indians, Mordechai replied that he had discovered the Indians were Jews. He said he chanced upon this discovery while a young man when an Indian tribe had let him participate in a green corn dance. At the end of the ritual, the Indians all shouted *"Yovohoka"* which means "Great Spirit" and, said Mordechai, obviously descends from the titles "Jehovah" and "Yahwe."

The rabbi did not pursue the point.

Enter the Immigrants

"WITH RESPECT to religion in its bearings upon political rights and privileges, no distinctions are recognized," wrote a Jewish immigrant to early America. "I find myself fully reimbursed for all the inconveniences of a toilsome journey by water and land." Another quotation, this time drawn from the works of one of the Founding Fathers: "May the wonder-working Deity who long since delivered the Hebrews from their Egyptian oppressors, planted them in a promised land, whose providential agency has lately been conspicuous in establishing these United States as an independent nation, still continue to

29

water them with the dews of heaven and make the inhabitants of every denomination participate in the temporal and spiritual blessings of that people whose God is Jehovah." George Washington was a bit muddled and wordy at times, but the sense of the above is recommended reading, at least in translation: "May the God who assisted the Jews in Egypt and helped the early years of the American Republic look with favor on all of us, of whatever religion, as he has done with his Chosen People."

The Jews of Europe came to America in three different waves of immigration, each one associated with a period of persecution or suppression in the Old World. The Inquisition of Spain and Portugal prompted an early exodus to America. These were the Sephardim, many of whom came to the United States by way of South America or the islands in the Caribbean. This influx occurred during the pre-Revolutionary days and continued during the early decades of the nineteenth century. By that time the Jewish community in America numbered approximately 15,000.

After 1840 they came from Germany—to escape repressive laws instituted by the various German governments. These German Jews were mostly peddlers and as such became a sort of mercantile American pioneer group. They eventually established large stores and went into the professions. Reform Judaism came to America with them.

The third and most numerous wave came from Russia to escape savage pogroms. The czars, fearing a popular revolution, had instituted official anti-Semitism in an attempt to distract attention from numerous political abuses. The laws continued in effect from the 1880's up to the Russian Revolution. President Benjamin Harrison expressed concern over the treatment the Jews of Russia were receiving, at the same time giving them a vote of confidence for their conduct in various nations: "The Hebrew is never a beggar; he has always kept the law—lives by toil—often under severe and oppressive civil restrictions. It is also true that no race, sect or class has more fully cared for its own than the Hebrew race." Theodore Roosevelt, following the Easter Massacre of Jews at Kishinev, Russia, likewise paid tribute to the character of this abused people: "I'd like to recall the admirable service which the Jews have rendered the American Republic. . . . I am most happy in the knowledge that the Jews were effective in the struggle for American independence and in the various wars of the Republic."

One of the newcomers to America associated with the second wave of immigration is worthy of mention here. He was Isaac Leeser, and he deserves our attention because of his devotion to an idea—a Jewish way of life in America. Leeser helped found Hebrew day schools, Hebrew College, and more than a dozen Jewish organizations. In addition, he was the founder of the Jewish-American press. In 1843 he founded the *Occident* and continued to edit this paper for twenty years. American Judaism found its voice in its pages. Isaac Leeser was also an author of textbooks and the founder of the seminary school Maimonides College.

During his youth, Leeser was a resident of Richmond, Virginia. His contributions to the Richmond *Whig* were his journalistic apprenticeship.

Why They Came

THEY CAME for commerce.

One of the first Jews to migrate to the South was Isaiah

Isaacs, who arrived in Virginia in 1782. Isaacs came because he wanted opportunity and because he was escaping surly creditors in London. A silversmith turned merchant and speculator, Isaacs formed a partnership with Jacob Cohen in Richmond. Cohen was also in the South for commercial and other reasons. A Philadelphian, Cohen had fallen in love with the widow Mordechai and made application to the synagogue to marry her. But Hester Mordechai had been Elizabeth Whitlock. She was a Christian who converted.

Romantically, Cohen left Philadelphia for Richmond, where he and the widow lived happily ever after. He and Isaacs speculated in land warrants which the legislatures of the thirteen colonies issued on lands expropriated from the Crown and from the Tories. Buying and selling these different warrants, which were for vast, ill-chartered and unknown tracts, was a speculative endeavor.

Most of the Jews who came to the South after the Civil War also came to do business. Enough Jews had come by the 1890's so that on the occasion of Rosh Hashonah, the Sanderson *Georgian* hailed the immigration with, "Where there are no Jews there is no money."

In Yanceyville, the Fels family operated a peddlers' warehouse. Most of the peddlers in the South operated with small capital, and few could afford trips to Baltimore or New York for supplies. The Felses were jobbers, and the father manufactured a soap of his own which he sold to peddlers. But he was able to manufacture this soap cheaply, so cheaply that he thought it would have a chance in the wide competitive market. Indeed the soap did well. The warehouse became the Fels Naphtha Company, and the money Joseph Fels accumulated from its success was used to endow Antioch College in Yellow Springs, Ohio, build a planetarium in Philadelphia and an observatory in Ohio. Joseph Fels also contributed several million dollars to the Henry George single tax movement.

There were no more than 40,000 Jews who came to the South between the Civil War and World War I. In the beginning, most of them were Germans—peddlers and small businessmen who wanted to embark on enterprise. Many of the Southern states commissioned agents to encourage immigration because the Civil War had devastated the South and left it with an inadequate and unreliable labor supply.

But two factors worked against extensive Jewish immigration. Jews from Eastern Europe had traveled a quarter of the globe by the time they reached New York. Many were loath to undertake another protracted journey to find a place to settle. By the time they reached New York they were by the hearth of *landsleit*.

Then, too, the South is xenophobic. While the governor and the industrialist may have wanted labor, the yeoman and the mill hand wanted to sustain the purity of their race. The South has always had a homogeneous white population that took its moral and physiological superiority for granted.

Wherever Jewish communities took root in the South, the Jews were in disproportionate numbers in commerce. One, two, or four of them would be directors of banks, active in reforming the Chamber of Commerce. They ran small factories producing products which ranged from harrows to crackers. And they were storeowners and shopkeepers. The Atlanta *Constitution* in 1890 congratulated their acumen

33

with the observation "Everyone must admire the wonderful business capacity with which the race seems imbued. . . ."

One of my first friends in Charlotte was Sanford Rosenthal, who made a comfortable living for many years buying yarn from the mills. Sanford bought the excess and discarded lots from one mill and then sold the same lots to another mill which could utilize it. What put Sanford out of business was the epidemic mergers of the small mills into the conglomerate. The conglomerate does its own wheeling and dealing not at all appreciative that Sanford paved the way. Don't worry about Sanford. He saw the handwriting on the wall. He was into realty and the stock market long before the Carolina Textile Company was a gleam in Dan River's eye.

The economy of the Jew in the South is based on self-employment. The 11,000-odd Jewish families of the two Carolinas represent to this day a single proprietary class of small capitalists, retailers, jobbers, wholesalers and manufacturers, traveling salesmen, and mill agents.

Out of such enterprise, of course, some men make money. My friend Moses Richter, of sainted memory, got into peaches. He owned several orchards in South Carolina. When the harvest came, Moses backed in boxcars, loaded and sent them north toward Washington or northwest toward Chicago. Moses sped to his Charlotte office whose four walls were blackboards, and several clerks stood by a battery of telephones charting in chalk the hourly price of peaches in every Northern market. If there was a half-cent difference per bushel between Albany and Providence, when the train got to Washington, Moses routed it to Rhode Island. Before the train pulled into the Pittsburgh terminal, Moses made his decision between Cincinnati and Cleveland markets.

I hesitate to say Moses was a genius. Certainly he was a superb administrator. For two decades he had that half-cent difference all to himself because the other orcharders always gave the engineer his destination when they gave him the manifest.

The Savannah Accession

FROM THE DECK of the *Pearl*, Benjamin Sheftall watched the early-morning sun burn away the sea fog that obscured the harbor. Behind the fog 10 miles inland on a bluff was the new English colony of Savannah, to which he and thirty-nine other Jews were bound.

Sheftall wondered about the reception they would meet. Nobody in Savannah expected the ship, let alone forty Jews to come ashore for the purpose of settling. Had anyone suspected such an intention, Sheftall and the other Jews crowded against the gunnels, also wondering, would still be living in London.

With the exception of Sheftall, an Englishman, though born in Germany, the other Jews were Portuguese who had fled to London to escape the Inquisition. They were the first Jews seeking refuge in a Crown colony.

By ability and inclination, Sheftall was the leader. He was more than literate; he was well educated and could keep books. While the others had sophisticated skills, Sheftall possessed the practical ones—carpentry, musketry, plumbing.

The sun was African when the Jews boarded the longboats. It was July 11, 1733. Ahead of the Jews was verdant Georgia.

Georgia was the first civilized attempt to solve the problem of welfare. The colony was the conception of James Edward Oglethorpe, a professional soldier and the son of a professional soldier. In 1731, Oglethorpe, a thirty-five-year-old member of the House of Commons, accepted the chairmanship of a commission to investigate conditions in English prisons.

The practice of imprisoning citizens for debt was by this time almost 500 years old, and the English were beginning to wonder to where it would all lead. Ten thousand Englishmen were serving indeterminate sentences because they owed other Englishmen money. Each year, as the figures swelled, the prisons bulged. The distinction between a debtor's prison and a felon's prison became more than blurred; it became nonexistent.

English prisons, Oglethorpe found, were uniformly infested with filth, vermin, smallpox, and fever. Mothers in cells bore children who perished. Jailers killed more debtors than they hanged thieves. Thumbscrews, floggings, shackles, and the iron skullcap were disciplinary measures meted out indiscriminately. Reforming a prison system was then no less than now an intractable proposition.

The way to alleviate prison conditions, Oglethorpe argued, was to get the debtors out of the prisons and into the colonies. He importuned his king, George II, for a Southern colony he would call Georgia whose climate would accommodate both plantations of mulberry trees for silk and vineyards for the fermentation of wines. He argued that a colony between the Carolinas and Florida would serve as a buffer against Spanish aggression.

"Give me Georgia," he promised, "and I will give England St. Augustine." *

* He never did. He failed to take St. Augustine in 1739 after England and Spain

Generously, George II gave Oglethorpe a jungle.

The charter Oglethorpe wrote contained four radical provisions:

It provided for the free exercise of religion of any sects, save Catholics.

It provided that land was not property.

It prohibited slavery.

And it prohibited rum, a prohibition which proved as futile in colonial Georgia as local option proved to industrial Georgia, lo! many years later.

To finance immigration, Oglethorpe established a charity governed by a board of trustees calling themselves the Common Council. The trustees empowered individuals, groups, and organizations to raise money to relieve the indebtedness of willing colonists and pay for their passage.

The colonization of Georgia, in the long run, did little to relieve the congestion of English prisons. As soon as the venture was made public, honest men up against hard times inundated the Common Council with petitions. The trustees screened every applicant, asking for testimony that he was worthy of English citizenship in a Crown colony.

It is a myth that Georgia was originally settled by the impecunious, the lawless, and the abandoned. The settlement on the Yamacraw was not peopled by renegades, nor was Savannah an earlier Botany Bay. Other English colonies were founded by individuals coming at will to advance their own fortunes, but in the beginning nobody came to Georgia without a certificate of good conduct.

On February 12, 1733, Oglethorpe set up the first colony in Georgia between the Savannah and Yamacraw rivers, choosing the spot because English settlers in Charleston

---

declared war, but he beat off the Spaniards from their incursion into the Carolinas at the Battle of Bloody Marsh in 1742.

pointed out it had the fewest swamps and might be malaria-free. There were no malaria epidemics in Savannah, but there was malaria.

Which was why the first settlers were happy to welcome the debarking Jews five months later. Among the Jews was a doctor, Samuel Nunez Ribiero, familiar with malaria and its remedies.

Sheftall, who spoke to Oglethorpe, listed the additional reasons for admitting Jews. None of the Jews was improvident. All had money. Some, in fact, had gold. One had even smuggled his silver tableware out of Portugal. All were willing to work.

The Jews were manpower. Oglethorpe was beginning to build the stockade and fort which would house the complement of soldiers. Only a few houses had been built, all of them close together to outline a grid for the city street. The rest of the settlers lived in bark-peeled cabins, a shelter they copied from the Indians which consisted of a ridgepole supporting several bent wooden ribs covered over with turf or bark, looking like a mound. Savannah needed men to build a town. Oglethorpe told Sheftall he was pleased to welcome Jews to the colony.

The trustees in London were not. The trustees were outraged. They had recently discovered that of the commissions they had dispensed empowering holders to solicit and receipt contributions, one had gone to three Jews: Alvaro Lopez Suasso, Francis Salvador, Jr., and Anthony Da Costa.

The sums raised were indeed handsome, but these Jews did not turn them over to the Common Council. Instead, they busied themselves collecting Hebrew colonists.

Consequently, the trustees instructed Oglethorpe not to admit the Jewish immigrants. They also issued a statement in which they promised the English public they would not make a Jews' colony of Georgia.

"This accession of Israelites," Oglethorpe called it in his reply, "far from proving a detriment has proved a boon."

For these people had appreciably increased the population of Savannah and had brought with them a doctor of which the colony was in sore need. They were thrifty, honest, and hardworking. Last, the Georgia charter provided for religious differences. To expel the Jews was to violate it.

The trustees compromised. They asked Oglethorpe to pay the doctor for his services but to see to it that no Jew shared in the grants of land within the province.

But in the general conveyance of lots, gardens, and farms, which was executed in December, 1733, several Jews did share, among them Abraham Minis, Isaac Nunes Henriques, Moses La Desma, Samuel Nunez, Abraham Monte Sano, and Benjamin Sheftall.

When the Salzburgers arrived in Savannah—seventy-eight German Protestants from the town of Berchtolgaden—they found the Jews already integrated within the English community. The diary of a Salzburger minister named Bolzius records his arrival in 1735 and notes that the Jews of the community relieved the inconvenience of the landing by inviting the Germans to their homes for a noon meal of rice soup.

To call Oglethorpe a "liberal" is an anachronism because the word in its popular meaning did not enter the language until the 1800's and then in a religious context. Let us say that Oglethorpe was a tenderhearted visionary. As a visionary, he realized that a practical race which wants to found a colony 3,000 miles away needs in that colony above all other things people. Whether people are indentured servants, English sirs, manumitted debtors, or Jews makes little difference as long as they are there. Without the Jews, the Salzburgers, Savannah might have become another Lost Colony. In 1740, George II natural-ized all the foreign Protestants and Jews who lived in America.

Oglethorpe's tenderheartedness did not cost him then, although it did later. George II ordered him court-mar-tialed in 1745 for failing to overtake and decimate fleeing Jacobite refugees. Oglethorpe was acquitted. In 1775, King George III offered him the command of the British armies in the colonies to put down the incipient rebellion. Ogle-thorpe agreed to accept this command if the king would also grant him powers of concession and conciliation, to which George III replied if he wanted a general to lose the war, he could lose one easily enough.

These first Jewish settlers in the South brought with them a scroll of the Law and a circumcision box, the gift of a London merchant named Lindo. A year to the day of their arrival, July 11, 1734, the first white child in Georgia was born, Philip Minis, who was later to lend the Continental Army $7,000. This child prompted the Jews to organize a synagogue, Mikvah Israel, which met thereafter in Shef-tall's two-room house.

The petulance of the trustees at the encroachment of the Jews dissipated when one of the new colonists showed them the way to quick profits. He was Abraham De Lyon. De Lyon was a skilled horticulturist, a *vineron* before fleeing Portugal. He had experimented with several varieties of grapes on the Georgia hillside and found the Portulan malaga grew in perfection. He proposed the trustees lend him 200 sterling for three years without interest to which he would add 200 of his own resources to import malaga vines from Portugal.

"Nothing has given me so much pleasure as what I have found here," wrote Colonel William Stevens, the agent of the trustees in 1737. "Though it is yet, if I may say so, only in miniature for De Lyon has cultivated only for two or three years past about half a score of these grapes which he received from Portugal. All bore fruit this year, very plentifully, a most beautiful large grape as big as a man's thumb, almost pellucid, in bunches exceedingly big."

Neither silk nor wine was a successful industry in Georgia because its climate often discouraged these products. Vineyards and orchards required many hands, and it was never profitable for more than one man and his family to work the land, although one man could manage vast tracts of land with slaves.

Some Jews worked in the mulberry orchards, some opened stores, and some became exporters and importers. What little we know of them we know from the diary Benjamin Sheftall kept in Hebrew which his sons continued in English.

According to the historians Charles M. Jones, Jr., and Leo Shpall, the diary is narrowly concentrated on the events in the lives of the Sheftalls and on the small triumphs and tribulations of Mikvah Israel. One of these triumphs was the founding of the Union Society, a colonial-day forerunner of the Community Chest, by the Jew Sheftall, the Catholic innkeeper Peter Tondee, and the Protestant Joshua Smith.

There were quarrels among the congregants, which is nothing new among Jews.

When Abraham De Lyon died, his family set aside a

small plot for a graveyard (which Savannah still calls the De Lyon Cemetery). When another of the founding Jews died, however, the De Lyon survivors said theirs was a private cemetery.

This smallness of heart annoyed the Jews.

Mordechai Sheftall, Benjamin's son, deeded a five-acre tract as a burial ground for all Jews, naming Isaac Da Costa, Levi Sheftall, and Philip Hart, of Charleston, merchants, overseers.

The most important event of Congregation Mikvah Israel in these early years was the exodus of most of the Jews in 1740. The Savannah colonials had that year petitioned the Common Council in London for the right to buy and sell land, an amendment to the charter they insisted would attract more settlers, and for the right to employ slaves within limits upon this land. One hundred and seventeen Georgians signed the petition. Yet when the Jews asked to be included, the colonials refused. The Jews promptly left for Charleston, Philadelphia, and New York. When the trustees said no to the petition, many of the Christians left, too.

Only three Jews remained in Savannah—Sheftall, De Lyon, and Minis. After Oglethorpe, the stumbling block, was recalled to England in 1743, the trustees reconsidered. They granted the petition. Curiously, they named among the commissioners to pass on applications from potential slaveholders Benjamin Sheftall and Abraham Minis. The colonists who hadn't allowed the Jews to sign the petition now had to await their okay. By 1750, most of the Jews of Mikvah Israel were back in Savannah.

Benjamin Sheftall died on October 3, 1767. He left three sons and a daughter, Sarah, who married a De Lyon. His eldest son, Mordechai, became prominent in the American

Revolution. He was one of the organizers of the Committee of Safety which broke open the British magazine to steal ammunition which the Patriots sent North to the men about to defend Bunker Hill. In fact, Mordechai was proscribed by the British as a "very great rebel" along with signers of the Declaration of Independence and two generals in Washington's army. As an afterthought, the proscription decreed all these men "ineligible to hold any office of dignity or trust."

When the active operations of the war shifted to the South, Mordechai Sheftall was commissioned by the Provisional Congress as commissary general for Georgia. He was charged with buying and issuing supplies for the Continental Army. His son, Sheftall Sheftall, fifteen, was his deputy.

In 1778 the British determined to capture Savannah and sweep north into the Carolinas. Late in December, Lieutenant Colonel Archibald Campbell landed men south of the city, led them through swamps, and routed a smaller American force under General Robert Howe.

Savannah fell. Mordechai and Sheftall, trying to flee, could not navigate Musgrove Creek, swollen by recent rains. Along with 186 other officers and men, they surrendered.

The British marched the prisoners through Savannah, past the courthouse to Mrs. Goff's store, which overlooked the bay and served as British headquarters. When Colonel Campbell discovered he had captured Mordechai Sheftall, he ordered him put under special guard. Gold Busler, the British commissary general, interrogated Sheftall in the process, boasting that Charles Town had fallen two weeks ago.

"Not so," said Sheftall, producing a letter from his brother written three days before.

"Good God," said Busler, "how you poor wretches are deluded by your leaders."

"If our leaders can deceive wretches," said Sheftall, "so can yours," a remark which so annoyed Busler he threw the two Sheftalls into a jail filled with drunken soldiers and blacks who, seeing gentlemen among them, spent the night threatening to skivver them.

Within the week, Sheftall and his son and the other American prisoners of war were embarked on the prison ship *Nancy*, bound for Antigua. The dismaying sight which greeted Mordechai Sheftall as he boarded were the writhings and moans of the wounded Continental soldiers who lay on the upper deck, many in their death throes.

After several weeks in a common jail in Antigua, the Sheftalls, among others, were released on parole to arrange a transfer of British prisoners of war for themselves. It was not an easy process, for the British made only qualitative trades, one commissary general for another. Jews in Philadelphia persuaded the Continental Army to release a redcoat general for the Sheftalls, and the British returned the father and son to Sunbury, Georgia.

In Philadelphia, the city to which the two Sheftalls repaired, the Board of War ordered the son to board the sloop *Carolina Packet*, which was to slip past the British blockade into Charles Town. There it would dock under a flag of truce and Sheftall would deliver food and money to American prisoners of war and their leader, General William Moultrie.

The money Sheftall delivered included guineas, Spanish pistoles, johannes, carlins, and silver dollars, an indication of how unstable the Continental currency was. His mission was successful. At least, General Moultrie is reported as having exclaimed, "Thank God, you've come."

Mordechai Sheftall died on July 6, 1797. Sheftall Sheftall survived his father by many years—until 1848. He practiced law in Savannah, where town folk called him cocked-hat Sheftall because he still affected the three-cornered hat and knickerbockers past the day tailors had made the fitted suit fashionable.

Dr. Moses Sheftall, a younger son of Mordechai, practiced medicine in Savannah and occupied a number of political offices in behalf of his constituency. He served as alderman, judge of the Superior Court, and a representative in the Georgia legislature.

The diary records that three great-grandchildren of Benjamin Sheftall—Laura, Mordechai, and Henry C.—died in the yellow fever epidemic which ravaged Savannah in 1854. Great-great-great-grandchildren of Benjamin still live in Savannah and in Gaffney, South Carolina, the descendants of a colonial who died twenty-two years before George Washington took the oath as the first President of the United States.

The first Jewish settlement in the South is important, however, not because it produced the Sheftalls and the Minises, although their history should serve as more than vanity for the American Jewish community, but because this Jewish community along the Yamacraw offers in microcosm perhaps the chief genesis of the Revolutionary War. The Jews were important not because they were Jews but because they were the dispossessed who, once settled in Savannah, became proprietors. In different contexts, with one shading or another, throughout the colonies the dispossessed came into possessions. People will often not revolt to save their lives but they will revolt to exploit their property.

Virginia and How the First Jews Came

IF THERE WERE any Jews in Virginia in 1740, not one took advantage of the Parliamentary Naturalization Act by which King George II conferred English citizenship on all Jews in the colonies.

Dr. John de Sequeyra, known also as Siccari, a crypto Jew, probably a Marrano, a convert who kept his origins a secret, was born in London in 1712. He came to Williamsburg in 1745 after being graduated as a physician from the University of Leiden in Holland.

He was, however, alone in Williamsburg because there was no reason for Jews to come to Virginia.

The Virginia landowners, the first settlers in the New World, were Cavaliers from England, the younger sons of noblemen and gentry who came to the colony with money to lay out estates like those they had known at home. They divided the country into domains over which each ruled as a manor lord. They were not interested in establishing mercantile centers for commerce. They needed no industry and therefore needed no city. The plantation society engendered no middle class.

By the eighteenth century the Virginia planter, now in his third and fourth generation, dominated economic, social, and political life. Unlike the other colonies, Virginia was of one mind about the Revolutionary War. The Cavaliers were Whigs who opposed continued allegiance to Great Britain. So effective was their control not only were there no Loyalist or Tory sentiments in Virginia, but there were no Loyalists or Tories.

No one who refused a sacrament of the Anglican Church in Virginia could be naturalized. These Anglican Cavaliers were like the Mohammedans—they taxed nonbelievers for not believing. One of the mainstays of the established Anglican Church in Virginia were tax revenues collected from dissident Protestants, particularly Baptists and Presbyterians. Sunday attendance at Anglican services was compulsory. Baptist and Presbyterian clergymen, and any Roman Catholic priest foolhardy enough to try, were not only prohibited from speaking on religious matters, but occasionally jailed.

Before the Revolutionary War, then, Virginia was no place for a boy from out of town.

The Revolutionary War brought profound changes, the first of which were legal. For the colonies, having declared independence, drew up their own constitutions. These democratic assemblies perpetuated nothing from English law. For example, all the states abolished primogeniture, the rights of the firstborn son to the property of a father who had died intestate. Virginia deposed the Anglican Church as the established church of the colony.

The Cavaliers were political. They were aware that the Revolution was the inspiration of the Virginia planters and New England businessmen. To succeed, the Patriots needed the resources, ardor, and manpower of all the other colonies most of which had established churches which happened not to be Anglican.

The Cavaliers also realized they needed Baptists and Presbyterians to fight in the militia which the state had to raise.

After the war, when the Virginians convened to establish a state church, it was too late. While the Anglicans were still in the majority, now there were other voices in the choir.

To make everyone happy, in 1784, the Virginia Assembly opted to establish the Christian religion as the state church.

Jefferson, Madison, Monroe, and Beverly Randolph, the Baptists, and Presbyterians argued that the General Assessment Plan for the Christian Religion would: (1) inhibit and deter immigration, thus stunting the natural growth of Virginia; (2) that it was inconceivable the Assembly could produce an all-inclusive definition of the Christian religion; (3) failing this definition, the Assembly was sooner or later condemning Christian to persecute Christian.

These considerations persuaded the legislature, which defeated the General Assessment Plan in 1785.

Jews were never the issue in this dialogue. Neither were the Catholics. The Baptists and the Presbyterians were the issue. When they prevailed, the Jews and the Catholics rode in on their coattails.

Thomas Jefferson filled the vacuum caused by the defeat of the General Assessment Plan with a bill establishing religious freedom for all which became law in 1786. Universal religious freedom made Virginia an anomaly among the states. Virginia was the one state which had enfranchised all its citizens before the Constitutional Convention met in 1787.

This triumph of reason in Virginia attracted at best two dozen Jews.

Which was a lot. At the end of the Revolutionary War there were 3,105 religious organizations in America, 5 of which—in Savannah, Charleston, Philadelphia, New York, and Newport—were Jewish. As late as 1825 there were only

6,000 Jews in America but they were collectively worth $10,000,000—which was also a lot.

In 1782 there were 3 Jews on the tax list of Richmond. In 1788 there were 25. By 1789, when the United States became the United States with ratification of the Constitution, there were enough Jews in Richmond to form a sixth congregation, Beth Shalom.

One of the first Jews to migrate to Virginia was Isaiah Isaacs. He came in 1782 seeking not to exercise his religious convictions but to escape creditors in London. He is often set in the pantheon of American Patriots because in his will, probated in 1806, he freed his slaves.*

Isaacs entered into a partnership with Jacob Cohen, who was also in Richmond for equally curious reasons. Cohen had lived most of his thirty-eight years in Philadelphia when, in 1782, he made formal application to the synagogue council of Mikvah Israel to marry the widow Mordechai. The application to the synagogue is *pro forma,* corresponding to Christian tradition of posting banns. The members of the synagogue council who processed Cohen's application should have fallen jointly to their knees. Moses Mordechai had left his widow not only bereft but with three small sons to share her bereavement, and the council had just advanced her nine pounds to pay her rent, with no relief in sight.

But Cohen's simple request became a *cause célèbre.* Hester Mordechai had been Elizabeth Whitlock before she mar-

* He wrote, "Being of the opinion that all men are by nature equally free and being possessed of these beings who are unfortunately doomed to slavery . . . my slaves are hereby manumitted and made free." He didn't however manumit the first of his slaves until 1820, fourteen years after he was dead. The last was to be freed in 1834, by which time Isaacs was sure his children would have enjoyed the use of their services. He manumitted any children of his slaves as soon as they turned thirty-one. I wonder what the life expectancy of a Virginia slave was in the early years of the nineteenth century.

ried, a Christian who had converted. The Halakah, the prescription of Jewish religious law, prohibits the marriage of a Cohen, whose name denotes he is a member of the priestly caste, a *kohanim*, with a divorcée or a convert. The council took the request under advisement.

Rabbi Gershom Seixas wrote the junta in London for permission to officiate at the ceremony. The junta, a collection of superannuated rabbis from Spain who knew little about the frontier and less about paying the rent of a poverty-stricken Jewish widow, instructed Seixas, "You are not to marry Mr. Cohen to Mrs. Mordechai. Neither are you to be present at the wedding. You are hereby strictly forbidden to mention said Cohen or his wife's name before the synagogue."

Jacob Cohen took this good enough reason to leave Philadelphia for Richmond, where he married the widow and lived happily ever after.*

Isaacs and Cohen were merchants who dealt primarily in tobacco, silverware, spices, and slaves. The firm also owned Richmond's oldest tavern, the Bird-in-Hand. But the bulk of their respective fortunes they made speculating in land warrants.

State legislatures had confiscated not only the lands of Tories, but all the lands owned by the Crown, vast, ill-charted tracts of land, often overlapping, stretching as far as the eye could see and farther (into the 1840's Connecticut owned a strip of Ohio which it finally ceded). This land was unexplored, uninhabited, and often impenetrable. The states used these lands to pay their debts, especially to the militiamen who had served in the war. Buying and selling these different warrants became a

---

* When he retired, Cohen returned to Philadelphia, where he became president no less of Mikvah Israel.

speculative industry. Land on a navigable river suddenly quadrupled. Land near a settlement quickly appreciated.

Unwittingly perhaps, speculators played a considerable role in opening up the West. Isaacs and Cohen, for example, hired Daniel Boone to explore and chart 10,000 acres for which they held warrants. They paid him an advance of six pounds specie. After Boone signed receipts for warrants and cash, Isaacs noted the transaction on the back of the receipt in Yiddish along with the date in 1783. Again, in 1784, they commissioned Boone to locate lands for them on the Licking River in Kentucky, a few miles south of present-day Cincinnati. Boone presented his bill to Isaacs and Cohen by messenger: "Send money by first opertunety. Mr. Samuel Grant, my sister's sun, will lykly hand you this letter. If so, he will be a good hand to send by and I will bee accountable for any money put into his hands unless kild by Indians."

Another Jew who came to Richmond in the 1780's was Meyer Derkheim, who yearly traversed all the Carolinas and Georgia, as well as Virginia. The eminent Jewish historian Jacob Rader Marcus, in his *Early American Jews*, remarks that any Jew who traveled extensively in these times was either a peddler, a *schnorrer* (beggar) or an itinerant mohel (circumciser). Derkheim was the latter. Circumcising does not provide a Jew with much of a living today, and it provided Derkheim with less then.

Derkheim also eked out a livelihood making candles and turpentine soap in a little shop opposite the State Capitol, and the Richmond town fathers paid him a small monthly stipend as the lamplighter for the bridge which crossed the creek at Main Street.

Rather than speculate, let us listen to what one Jew thought about other Jews in Virginia. She is Rebecca, the

51

wife of Hyman Samuels, who came with him to Petersburg when he opened a silversmith shop and described how she lived to her parents in Hamburg, Germany:

> . . . The Jews of Newport and New York when they hear the name Virginia, they get nasty. It won't do for a Jew. In the first place it is an unhealthful district and we are only yeomen. . . . You cannot imagine what kind of Jews they have here in Virginia. Most are German itinerants who made a living by begging in Germany. They came to America as soldiers and now they can't recognize themselves. One can make a good living here and one can live in peace. One can do what he wants. Jew and Gentile are as one. There is no *galut* [exile]. In New York and Philadelphia, there is more *galut*. The reason is that there are too many German Gentiles and Jews there. The German Gentiles cannot forsake their anti-Jewish prejudice and the German Jews cannot forsake their disgraceful conduct and that's what makes the *galut*.

Two years later, in 1791, she wasn't as equable about the lack of *galut:*

> . . . I know quite well you would not want me to bring up my children as Gentiles. Here they cannot become anything else. This is a Christian society here. There are here in Petersburg 10 or 12 Jews and they are not really called Jews. We have a *schokhet* [ritual butcher] who goes to market and buys *trefa* [nonkosher food]. On Rosh Hoshanna and Yom Kippur, the people worship here without one *sefer* [Torah scrolls]. And not one wore the *tallit* [ritual prayer cloth], except my Sammy's godfather. He has been in America for 30 years. For 20 years he was in Charleston and he has been living here for 4 years. He does not want to remain here any longer and he will go with us to Charleston. In that place, there is a blessed community of 300 Jews. You can believe that I crave to see a synagogue to which I can go. We do not know what the Sabbath and the Holidays are. On the Sabbath, all the Jewish

shops are open and they do business on that day as they do throughout the week. We do not allow ours to open so with us there is some Sabbath. As for the Gentiles, we have nothing to complain about. For the sake of a livelihood, we do not have to leave here. Nor do we have to leave because of debts. You cannot know what a wonderful country this is for the common man. People can live here peacefully. Hyman made a clock that goes very accurately just like the one in the Buchenstrasse in Hamburg. Now you can imagine what honors Hyman has been getting here. In all Virginia there is no clock like this one and Virginia is the greatest province in all America and America is the largest section of the world.

Imagine! in Virginia, in 1791, a *yenta*.

The Jews of Early Georgia

In 1733 King George II granted a charter to General Oglethorpe to found the colony of Georgia in the New World. Scarcely a few months had passed after Oglethorpe had landed and set up the community of Savannah when a shipload arrived from England bearing forty new colonists—all Jews.

Consternation! Since the new community consisted of scarcely more than a few hundred souls, the new influx threatened, to quote the words of the protest issued by the trustees of Savannah, "to make a Jews' colony of Georgia."

How had the disaster happened?

Investigation showed that the trustees themselves were indirectly responsible. In an effort to attract money and settlers to the colony of Georgia, the trustees (appointed by the king) had granted commissions to three of the wealthiest Jews in England—Salvador, Suasso, and Da Costa, director of the Bank of England. These gentlemen had promptly sniffed freedom, gathered forty landsmen, outfitted a ship, paid all the expenses, and sent the ship on its way.

Salvador, Suasso, and Da Costa had acted without the knowledge of the trustees, who later were outraged and demanded the surrender of the commissions. The three aforementioned gentlemen refused to oblige them.

Meanwhile, Oglethorpe had received instructions not to "encourage" the newcomers, to see "that they be allowed no kind of settlement with any of the grantees," etc. Oglethorpe replied to the effect that the Jews were an asset to the colony, especially one Dr. Samuel Nunez, who had served the needs of colonists admirably. The trustees wrote back and said, fine, give Dr. Nunez a "gratuity," but under no circumstances should any Jew be given a land grant in Georgia.

Oglethorpe paid no attention. The records show that several of the Jewish settlers were given land grants before 1773.

One of the grantees was Abraham De Lyon, a vintner from Portugal, who attracted much attention with his skill at growing grapes imported from the old country.

Soon after the first shipment, another boatload of Jews landed in Georgia, this time without protest. Even before the first year of the new colony had drawn to a close, one-third of the settlement of Savannah was Jewish.

The Jews promptly established a reputation for honesty and hard work. Oglethorpe founded a Masonic lodge, which included several of the Jewish settlers in its membership. In 1751 the Jews helped organize a public library. The Union Society, an interfaith organization still in existence, was founded in 1750 and exemplifies the harmony between faiths in pre-Revolutionary Georgia. By the nineteenth century Jews had served with distinction in the political, professional, and social life of the state.

A story is still told which illustrates the interpretation of Jewish and Gentile fortunes in Georgia. A few years after Abraham Simons, a wealthy merchant of Wilkes County, died, his widow married a Baptist preacher named Jesse Mercer. At the demise of Mrs. Mercer, the good reverend inherited the Simons' fortune, which he used to endow a new school, which to this day bears his name. It is now Mercer University, the leading Baptist seminary in the South, with 400 students. In 1911 the report of the Baptist Mission Board stated: "Mercer University is largely indebted to the skill and enterprise of a Jewish financier for much of the larger part of its life and power. A copious Providence this, which founds a Christian college on Jewish cornerstones."

The American Revolution and the Jews in Virginia

THE JEWS of early Virginia played a considerable role in the American Revolution. Simon Nathan lent money to the state of Virginia, while Captain Jacob Henry headed up a cavalry company which saw action at the Battle of Jamestown.

Prior to the Revolution there are few but significant references to the part played by Jewish settlers in Virginia's history. Michael Franks and Jacob Myer served with Washington on one of his early campaigns into Ohio, while Michael Israel was a border ranger and member of the militia in Albemarle County. Because of his real estate holdings and dealings, a mountain pass near Albemarle is still called Israel's Gap. One Hezekiah Levy belonged to the same lodge in Fredericksburg that counted George Washington among its membership.

In Richmond following the Revolution, the Jewish community founded the Amicable Society to Help Strangers in Distress. Jacob Mordecai, Samuel Noah, Jacob Cohen, and Moses Myers were among the distinguished Jews of Richmond during the post-Revolutionary period. Noah was a graduate of West Point who served in the War of 1812. Cohen, who fought in the Revolution, became a Richmond magistrate. And Moses Myers became superintendent of the Bank of Richmond. He is accorded space in William Forrest's *Eminent and Representative Men of Virginia*. In the 1780's Dr. Isaac Levy practiced medicine in Virginia and is remembered today for his generous contributions to the Virginia treasury, as well as his part in a curious and amusing lawsuit. Seems Dr. Levy took one of his patients to court for nonpayment of bills. The patient complained that he had not been cured and that payment was therefore unwarranted. The court directed Dr. Levy to continue treatment. Later the case was reopened when the doctor brought suit again, claiming that his patient refused to follow doctor's orders. The patient explained that he took sixty pills in two days instead of seven pills in one day, so that he could be cured more speedily. When Dr. Levy demonstrated that sixty pills of the sort prescribed would be lethal, the court decided in his favor.

Religious freedom was guaranteed in the Virginia Constitution, the author of the clause being none other than Thomas Jefferson, who had his part in the transaction memorialized on his tombstone.

The Three Years of Colonist Francis Salvador

IN 1773 Francis Salvador, aged thirty-five, arrived in the British colony of South Carolina. He had come from Twickenham, England, where he had left his family, to invest his time and resources in the New World. Francis Salvador was descended from the Salvador who had encouraged the first Jewish settlers of early Georgia. His father, who had died when Francis was two, had purchased land in America, had added to the family fortune, and had left Francis some 60,000 pounds sterling.

Francis Salvador purchased a large estate in South Carolina and settled in. He made friends quickly—men with names like Pinckney and Rutledge. A year after his arrival, Salvador was sitting in the South Carolina General Assembly.

The year following, 1775, a Provincial Congress was set up at Charleston, and Salvador was sent as a delegate from his district. Among other things the Congress drafted a list of grievances to be presented to the royal governor, who received the list and ignored it. After the Battle of Lexington, the second Congress was convened with Salvador once again participating, this time more actively than before.

In 1776 Salvador raised the alarm against Indian allies of Great Britain, who had just descended upon Charleston in a bloody assault encouraged by the British. In 1775 and 1776 Francis Salvador was a familiar revolutionary of the area: He made speeches that were fiery enough to enrage some of the colony's Loyalists, who were not yet aroused to

57

the inevitable. Nonetheless Salvador recruited 500 volunteers for the cause.

In July, 1776, Salvador and Major Williamson led the new militia on campaigns against the Tories and their Indian allies. Early in August Salvador was killed in a skirmish between the Patriots and the Indians. A chronicler of the period observed that his loss was "regretted by the whole army, as he was universally loved and esteemed." Francis Salvador was 38 at the time of his death, and he had been in the New World just three years.

Thus Francis Salvador may be said to have been the first Jew to fall in defense of our country.

Winning Their Rights

IN 1668, when the Ukrainian Bogdan Chmielnicki massacred more than a half million Jews in Eastern Europe, the English philosopher John Locke wrote the Constitution for the Crown colony of South Carolina which conferred upon the citizens "in as ample a manner as they might desire" freedom of religion and conscience. In 1776, when Frederick the Great restricted the number of marriages between Jews to 300 a year (and then only on the condition the newlyweds would buy chinaware from the royal porcelain factory), Thomas Jefferson wrote the Declaration of Independence.

These ideals broke the back of the Middle Ages. They divorced the New World from the afflictions of antiquity. It is important to remember that the statement of these ideals did not mean immediate or practical implementation either in 1668 or in 1776. Or for that matter in 1974. But the ideals became the law to which all had recourse in the United States.

The Jews of Europe were, until the advent of Hitler, always involved in negotiating for special privileges, privileges enjoyed by one class of Jews not dispensed to other Jews. The American ideal ended the "host-guest" relationship. It ended negotiating. In the South Jews *sued* for their rights; they did not—and could not—have won them by persuasion.

The Jews have had pretty smooth sailing in Savannah ever since *qua* Jews. The British invested it in 1779, and so did Sherman in 1864, neither of the occupations pleasant episodes. Typhoid epidemics ravaged the population for a century.

Though the Ku Klux Klan was born in Georgia, Klansmen never intimidated Savannah Jews. Part of the reason is that Savannah is a great port city and consequently more cosmopolitan than many Southern cities, and part of the reason is that Savannah has a large Irish Catholic population (the Church of St. John the Baptist on Abercorn Street by Lafayette Square is the cathedral of the Bishop of Georgia). From the 1900's on the Jews and the Irish in Savannah made political cause together. The Jews are no longer so active, having come to the conclusion that politics is no way for a Southern boy to make money.

The Revolutionary War brought many changes. The Cavaliers were politic. They were aware that the Revolution was the inspiration of the Virginia planters and New England businessmen. To succeed, the Patriots needed the resources, ardor, and manpower of other colonies, most of whom had established churches which happened not to be Anglican. The Cavaliers also realized they needed Baptists and Presbyterians to fight in the Virginia militia.

After the war, when the Virginians convened to establish a state church, it was too late. While the Anglicans were still in the majority, now there were other voices in the choir. In 1784, the Virginia Assembly opted to establish the Christian religion as the state church.

These considerations persuaded the legislators who defeated the General Assessment Plan in 1785.

Thomas Jefferson filled the vacuum with a bill establishing religious freedom for all which became law in 1786. Universal religious freedom made Virginia an anomaly among the states. Virginia was the one state which had enfranchised all its citizens before the Constitutional Convention met in 1787.

This triumph of reason in Virginia attracted at best two dozen Jews.

Which was a lot. In 1782 there were three Jews on the tax list of Richmond. In 1788 there were twenty-five. By 1789, when the United States became the United States with ratification of the Constitution, there were enough Jews in Richmond to form the sixth congregation in the new country, Beth Shalom.

The First Kennedy

IN 1625, King Charles I gave George Calvert, the first Lord Baltimore, all of Newfoundland. Calvert didn't want Newfoundland, a cold place. Charles reconsidered. In 1632 he gave Calvert a patent on Mary Land, named after the queen, Henrietta Maria. Calvert died before the patent was secured, but it passed to his son, Cecilius Calvert, the second Baron Baltimore.

Cecilius Calvert hoped to increase his business interests by establishing a settlement in Maryland, but he also hoped to provide a refuge for fellow Catholics.

The last paragraph of the king's charter warned the new lord proprietor that nothing was to be admitted to the colony "by which God's Holy and Truly Christian religion may in any thing suffer any prejudice or diminution." When Cecilius Calvert and his brother, Leonard, who governed Maryland, recruited the first colonists, they made sure to include two boatloads of Protestants. For fifteen years Catholics and Protestants lived in amity in St. Mary's, the first settlement in Maryland, even sharing the same chapel.

More and more Puritans, however, came down to Maryland from the other colonies, and the Puritans were gaining ascendancy in England.

When William of Orange succeeded to the English throne in 1689, Catholics suffered. They suffered in the colonies, too. In 1692 Maryland made the Church of England the established church of the colony, and in 1702 the legislature enacted a law which provided that residents pay the local minister in tobacco. In 1718 the legislature proscribed Catholics from holding public office and effectively disenfranchised them.

The Revolutionary War erased differences. Once the colonies declared independence, they drew up their own constitutions in which they perpetuated little from English law. They abolished primogeniture, for example, the right of the firstborn son to the estate of his father, and they disestablished the Anglican Church. The Maryland Constitution, written in 1776, recognized the duty of every man to worship God "in such manner as he thinks most acceptable to Him; all persons professing the Christian religion are

61

equally entitled to protection in their religious liberty. No other test or qualification ought to be required on admission to any office of trust or profit than such oath and support of fidelity to the State and a declaration of belief in the Christian religion."

The historian Isaac M. Fein in *The Making of an American Jewish Community* writes: "It is doubtful whether the handful of Jews in the colony objected to this qualification. True, it was a discriminatory law, but it did not affect any of them. None of them aspired to a government position. They were strangers, and all they wanted was the opportunity to be left alone to make a living."

By 1790, however, at least one of the fifty Jews in Baltimore was concerned.

The Jew, Solomon Etting, who, in 1797, with his father-in-law, Bernard Gratz, sent a petition to the legislature noting that they were "a sect of people called Jews and thereby are deprived of invaluable rights of citizenship and praying to be placed on the same footing as other good citizens."

Solomon was the son of Shinah Etting, a widow who moved a family of five daughters and two sons to Baltimore from York, Pennsylvania, after her husband's death in 1780. She started a boardinghouse at Market and Calvert streets which became a famous ornament in the city. In 1790 Solomon opened a hardware store. Six years later he was a director of the Union Bank, and eventually he was to become a director of the Baltimore and Ohio Railroad.

Etting petitioned several times more and in 1804 was joined by Jacob Cohen, also the son of a widow, Judith Cohen, who had settled in Baltimore in 1803. The Cohen family ran a lottery which was one of the ways to accumulate funds for investment. Eventually, the lottery became a bank, the house of Jacob I. Cohen and Brothers, the agents for the Rothschilds in the United States.

There were compelling reasons for Etting and Gratz to petition for these rights. They were men of substance, rich by the standards of their time, and they wanted the rights as well as the privileges of rich men. They wanted the right to pursue their interests politically. They were also native-born Americans who disliked the stamp of alien. While they themselves were businessmen, they may have entertained other ambitions for their sons.

The legislators listened politely to the Jews and promptly buried the petition in committee.

The Ettings, the Gratzes, and the Cohens might have gone on forever importuning the legislature—Jews were not enfranchised in North Carolina until 1868—were it not for a Kennedy, not from Ireland, but from Scotland. Thomas Kennedy was born in Paisley, Scotland, in 1776, the son of William, a farmer. His older brother, Matthew, had emigrated from Scotland to America, and Thomas Kennedy, growing up, read glowing descriptions of the New World and cultivated a romantic desire to live in the land of freedom and "to spend my life in virtuous service for freedom's cause." There was no Jewish vote in Baltimore. The Jews there did not, in fact, found a synagogue in Baltimore until 1830, and then it was populated by the immigrants arriving from Western Europe.

He embarked at Glasgow on the *Britannia* and thirty-eight days later landed at Georgetown on the Potomac. The ship fired a salvo as it dropped anchor which summoned the residents from their homes and shops and farms to the wharf. Kennedy was the first passenger out of the captain's jollyboat, and the first person he met was his older brother, Matthew, whom he had not seen in eleven years. The event

63

deserves mention not because of its singularity but because it tells us how small some American ports were.

"After drinking some Republican whiskey," Kennedy wrote, "I sat at my brother's table in peace."

Later Matthew took his brother to what was to become the new capital city, Washington, which was then, Kennedy wrote, "a wilderness." The White House was not completed, and the Capitol had as yet no roof. The streets were muddy paths.

Thomas Kennedy found a job as a bookkeeper for a Georgetown merchant and later for the contractor who put the bridges across the Potomac. He loved sightseeing and on a visit to Niagara met Miss Rosalind Toms of Frederick. A few years later, he married her and moved to Hagerstown, where he founded a newspaper, the Hagerstown *Mail*.

He was a man of medium height, portly, with blue eyes. He wrote poetry almost as long-winded as his speeches which, if not templates of rhetoric, were vessels of patriotism.

In 1817 he was elected to the state legislature, as a representative from Washington County. He took his new duties seriously. He applied himself to a close reading of the United States Constitution and to the constitutions of other states. He discovered the disabilities legally visited upon the Jews by the Maryland Constitution.

Kennedy was a man looking for a cause. He had found one. He resolved to right this wrong. His opponents argued that the property of Jews was safeguarded, their lives were protected, their opportunity to earn a fortune guaranteed; why must they persevere in seeking the right to hold office?

"It is my duty," said Kennedy. It is as simple a statement as he ever made.

On December 9, 1818, Kennedy introduced a resolution

calling for the appointment of a committee "to consider the justice and expedience of placing the Jewish inhabitants on an equal footing with the Christian." Appointed to this committee, of which Kennedy was chairman, were Henry Brackenridge, a judge from Baltimore, and Ebenezer Thomas from Baltimore County. The committee submitted a report in which it concluded there was only one side to the subject: In a democratic society, legislatures must determine civil, state, and military duties, but as for religion there is no law which can reach a man's heart and no human tribunal has a right to take cognizance of this matter. The committee went on to introduce an act to confer upon Jews the same rights conferred by the constitution on all citizens of Maryland. It was popularly known as the Jew Bill or Kennedy's Jew Baby.

The legislature debated the bill the next year.

Kennedy argued: "I am free to declare that if Christianity cannot stand without the aid of persecution, let it fall; and let a new system, more rational and more benevolent, take its place."

It was not the appropriate sentiment to press upon men who took going to church seriously.

The bill lost, 50 to 24.

The Jew Bill became an inflammatory issue in which, curiously, the Jews were only incidental. Nativism was beginning to sink its roots in the American subsoil. With the end of the Napoleonic Wars in Europe, immigration to America began in earnest, and rural, agrarian communities worried about foreigners taking over the government. There was also a crucial issue in the American constituency between the Jeffersonians and the Federalists, the argument between democratic home rule and a strong, centralized government, an issue which centered on tariffs, taxes, and the minting of currency. Maryland was Federalist, and the vote for or against the Jew Bill was determined by party lines.

In fact, controversy over the Jews of Maryland in the 1800's much resembled the controversy over fluoride in the 1950's. If you wanted Congress to repeal the Fifth Amendment in order to flush out subversives, you automatically did not want to fluoridate the municipal reservoirs. If you wanted to protect civil rights, you were in favor of fluoridation. In Maryland of 1819 if you wanted your party to control the state and distribute patronage, you automatically had to restrain Jews from running for public office. Kennedy had lit upon one of those minor issues which delight legislators, an issue on which men could uphold or sacrifice their principles without risking much.

In 1822, Kennedy came back for more. This time he introduced a broader bill, "An Act to extend to the citizens of Maryland the same civil rights and privileges that are enjoyed under the Constitution of the United States."

Kennedy was learning. Machiavelli advises the Prince never to tell his ministers there is a thorny and difficult problem awaiting their solution; instead, the Prince must tell them there is an easy solution awaiting their signature. The way to pass a Jew Bill, Kennedy discovered, was by a constitutional amendment which subtracted Jews from the issue.

The legislature passed it. But because the act involved a constitutional amendment, the succeeding legislature had to confirm it.

Thomas Jefferson wrote letters to the newspapers urging passage. Jacob Cohen, in a letter to Ebenezer Thomas, reminded everyone, "In time of peril and war the Jews had borne the privation incident to such times in defense of the common cause." All of which helped the opponents connect the Jews to the act. They mustered the strength to defeat it, charging that the defenders of the Jews were a menace to the community and anti-Christian.

In the election of 1823, Kennedy was in serious trouble with his constituency. He was accused of being an enemy of Christianity, a Judas Iscariot. His opponent, Benjamin Calloway, running on the Christian ticket, said he "deprecated any change in our state government calculated to afford the least chance to enemies of Christianity."

Kennedy was defeated.

But he won again in 1825, and this time the amendment passed. This time the Jews played a more active and vigorous role. They presented another petition, this one signed by Solomon Etting, Jacob Cohen, and Levi Solomon.

The Baltimore newspapers supported the bill. And the national press urged passage. The Catholics in Maryland also favored its enactment.

It passed 26 to 25, with 80 legislators abstaining or absent.

The amendment required every citizen appointed or elected to any office of public trust to swear to defend the Constitution of Maryland and the United States and "make and subscribe a declaration of his belief in a future state of rewards and punishments."

By a vote of 45 to 32 the amendment was confirmed in January, 1826. Later in the year Solomon Etting and Jacob Cohen became the first Jews elected to office in Maryland when they won seats on the Baltimore City Council.

John Quincy Adams made Kennedy the postmaster general of Hagerstown in 1828, a post Kennedy held for four years until he died of Asiatic cholera in 1832. Outside

Hagerstown is an obelisk dedicated by Baltimore Jews to Kennedy's memory.

The crucial fact about the Jew Bill in Maryland and about the antagonism it engendered is that throughout, it was a political fight. Catholic sentiment favored the Jews. Protestant sentiment may not have been enthusiastic, but clergymen remained noncommittal. One of the reasons the Jews did win the right to hold public office was that the issue was not religious. The fight against the Jews was led by politicians and legislators, not by ministers and priests; by people who may or may not have known what they were talking about rather than the people whose interests were directly at stake. The observation was made more succinctly in 1831 by the Frenchman Alexis de Tocqueville, in Volume I of *Democracy in America*. He writes, "It may be asserted then, that in the United States no religious doctrine displays the slightest hostility to democratic and republican institutions. The clergy of all different sects there hold the same language, their opinion is in agreement with the laws and the human mind flows onward, so to speak, in one undivided current."

Atlanta, Georgia

THERE WERE JEWS in the South before there was a South. Spanish and Portuguese Jews from the Barbados established the indigo trade in the Carolinas as early as 1720.

There were Jews in Atlanta before there was an Atlanta. Jacob Haas came to America from Germany in 1803, settled in Georgia in a town called Marthasville, later renamed Atlanta. A daughter, Caroline, born to the Haas family, was the first white girl to be born in the newly named city. And this may come as a surprise to many people; nowhere in America was the Jew received with greater generosity.

Atlanta is the miracle city of the South. Its progress industrially, politically, and economically has been phenomenal.

Rabbi David Marx, a legendary figure of Atlanta, was the spiritual head of the Temple for fifty-one years, having arrived in September, 1895. Rabbi Marx was a tower of strength in the building of the new temple and in building a high prestige of the Jewish community.

By his ability, Rabbi Dr. Marx in effect became the congregation not only to the Christian world but to his own members as well.

Atlanta has a population of 850,000. There are 25,000 Jews in Atlanta. The Jewish community is not fleeing to the suburbs. The geographical shift of the population, as for instance, clearance of the space around the stadium for this purpose, moves to the northeast.

There are two Jewish social clubs, one in midtown, the Progressive Club, and the country club, the Standard Club, complete with golf course.

The third club closed, the Mayfair Club, which was destroyed by accidental fire. The property was sold at a fabulous price to the surprise of the stockholders who had to ante up to join and never expected to get a fair price, much less a margin of profit out of it.

The Atlanta Jewish Community Center has a lovely and spacious building, close to which the Federation of Jewish Philanthropies has now erected quarters. The AJCC only recently enlarged its gym facilities, etc. It operates a day camp, Zaban Park and Camp Barney Medintz, at Cleveland, Georgia.

While a century ago the Jewish population was probably mostly German Jewry, through the years this has changed, and for this century the influx was from every source from which the immigrants came—Russia, Poland, Rumania, France, England, Isle of Rhodes—even lately a trickle from the Arab countries, including Egypt.

The anti-Zionist attitude has indeed disappeared, and the general attitude of Atlanta Jewry toward Israel is overwhelmingly enthusiastic with an identification that is quite wholesome and marvelous. Among the community leaders are such individuals as Milton Weinstein, president of Atlanta Jewish Welfare Federation, and Dr. Irving and Marvin Goldstein, brothers, dentists, and outstanding in about all facets of communal life; Dr. Irving Freenberg, surgeon, and particularly outstanding in Jewish education; Sidney Feldman, son of a founder of Farband in Atlanta, Federation VP; Larry Frank and Jerry Dubroff; Dr. William S. Schatten (the new young breed); Dr. Herbert Karp, physician, Zionist, member of Emory Medical School Faculty; Dr. Mike Mescom, Georgia State University professor; Joel Goldberg, president of Rich's; Mrs. Sidney Janus, president of the Georgia League of Women Voters; and many others, including Elliott Levitas and Sidney Marcus, Georgia state legislators.

A thousand or more are in universities and colleges through the state; the actual figures are unavailable. Many faculty members, including professors of national and international repute, particularly Dr. Robert Greenblatt, world-famous endocrinologist and teacher at UGA med school at Augusta.

Two men are essentially responsible for this miracle of
Atlanta, former Mayor William B. Hartsfield and editor
Ralph McGill. Atlanta had Ralph McGill and the *Constitution*, and Birmingham, Alabama, had Bull Connor and the
police dogs.

The difference between Ralph McGill and Bull Connor
is the difference one man can make. Atlanta is a city of
reason, and Birmingham is a city that literally should arrest
itself.

It wasn't easy. The night Ralph McGill's wife lay dying
someone fired a shot through his living-room window.
When Ralph McGill wrote an editorial, Southerners called
him "Rastus."

Ralph McGill is dead, and Atlanta is poorer for it. Bull
Connor still strides the streets of his hometown, and I
wonder how many industries and government agencies
have said we cannot locate there.

Ralph McGill championed integration in the very city
Sherman considered the heart of the Confederacy. Sherman
burned the city. Atlanta was the very city which gave birth
to the Ku Klux Klan. Three times Atlanta has had race
riots that beggar all description. Yet there was one man. As
Clarence Darrow said, "There is always that one man who
says no."

Ralph McGill said no since 1929. And Ralph won.
Ralph said no in the city which once considered an
ordinance requiring builders to install segregated elevators
and windows.

He said first the separation of races by law is wrong and
unchristian; he said next the South denies itself a vast
wealth by insisting on such.

When he joined the Atlanta *Constitution* more than thirty

years ago, Atlanta prided itself on the Five Corners and on the old folks who could show a visitor the streets through which Sherman's bummers marched.

When he died a few years ago, Atlanta had a skyline, the third largest on the Eastern seaboard. It is the richest city in the South, and it is the city that led the fight for reapportionment, winning that fight in the Supreme Court.

Atlanta is a cut above the national Jewish average, Atlanta Jews being pacers in Southern race relations improvements.

Two of the most significant developments of late decades are the development of day school education and the presence of Israelis. The Hebrew Academy (grammar school), with 250 students, continues to grow. There is even a Yeshiva High School, with a tiny enrollment of less than a dozen (expensive per pupil and totally religious as opposed to the nondenominational emphasis, but yet decidedly Jewish bilingual Academy). The other fort has been the presence of Israelis, as students at Atlanta and Georgia colleges and universities, as students in Atlanta's synagogue and academy classes, and the highlight arrival of the consul Nahum Aster, as the first of a succession of dynamic and fantastic representatives of the Israeli story. This—the establishment of the regional consulate—was followed by establishment of the Tourist Office, the Aliyah office, and lately El Al Airlines. All have been the focuses of much Israeli- and Jewish-oriented activities and emphasis.

There has been some evidence of black anti-Semitism, most flagrant from the Panther types or militants. Jewish merchants in black areas have had a rough time and in many instances been forced to give up. The amount however has on the whole been insignificant, according to an Anti-Defamation League informant.

72

Mixed marriages continue to be a problem, probably no more than in other areas. Local rabbis try to discourage intermarriages and refuse to preside at marriages, unless there has been a conversion. These have been frequent, and the Temple at least has periodic classes to help instruct and guide the participants, before and after marriage. Only two Georgia rabbis to my knowledge perform intermarriages— one in Augusta and one in Albany.

Judaism has an attraction for young Jews of Atlanta. It seems to be more realistic and less euphoric with such identifiable things as a Jewish state and the general world reaction to the holocaust.

The Atlanta Federation charities reached its goal in 1972 of $5,500,000. For United Jewish Appeal purposes, $3,500,000, and for Bonds of Israel (another campaign) $2,000,000.

It is remarkable that a city which had produced a mob that hanged Leo Frank in 1915 should have elected a Jew as a mayor.

On the morning of October 12, 1958, the Temple's longtime custodian, Robert Benton, arrived as usual at 7:15 A.M. to open the building and prepare it for religious school. To his horror he discovered that the building had already been opened by a twenty-foot hole in its side wall, later determined to have been blasted there by some forty to fifty sticks of dynamite. At ten o'clock, the time religious school classes normally began, the Temple congregation of Atlanta was front-page news around the world.

The blast was more than a shock. It was a shock treatment. For Jew and non-Jew alike the bomb released long-buried thoughts about themselves and each other. It blasted through the Southern moderates' wall of silence. All "the right people," from Georgia Governor Marvin Griffin to President of the United States Dwight D. Eisenhower, had "the right thing to say" about the bombing and said it for publication. Messages of sympathy poured in, many accompanied by monetary offerings, even though the fact was repeatedly broadcast that the building was adequately insured.

But the real significance of the bombing had nothing to do with physical damage or physical repair. Atlanta Mayor William B. Hartsfield, arriving at the temple within minutes of hearing the news, pointed it out immediately. "Looking at this demolition," he declared, "I cannot help but realize it is the end result and payoff of a lot of rabble-rousing in the South. Whether they like it or not, every political rabble-rouser is the godfather of these cross burners and dynamiters who sneak about in the dark and give a bad name to the South. It is high time that decent people of the South rise and take charge if governmental chaos is to be avoided." This sounded the call. The good people of the South did arise and speak out.

The most eloquent voice was one long accustomed to speaking out, and one which Southerners were long accustomed to hearing. Ralph McGill, in a column which would help him win the Pulitzer Prize, said:

> Let us face the facts.
> This is a harvest. It is the crop of things sown.
> It is the harvest of defiance of courts and the encouragement of citizens to defy law on the part of many Southern politicians. . . .
> It is not possible to preach lawlessness and restrict it.
> To be sure, none said go bomb a Jewish temple or a school.
> But let it be understood that when leadership in high places in any degree fails to support constituted authority, it opens the gates to all those who wish to take law into their hands.

It is a harvest, too, for those so-called Christian ministers who have chosen to preach hate instead of compassion. Let them now find pious words and raise their hands in deploring the bombing of a synagogue.

You do not preach and encourage hatred for the Negro and hope to restrict it to that field. . . .

Quite a different reaction from that which greeted members of the Hebrew Benevolent Congregation in 1915! While many factors had changed in Georgia between the Frank case and the Temple bombing, until the bombing many Temple members did not realize it.

When President Dwight D. Eisenhower learned of it, he called the Confederate Underground, an organization which boasted it had set the bomb, "a bunch of Al Capone gangsters."

A bomber *was* arrested and charged with the crime. George Bright twice faced a jury accused of serving as a lookout. The first jury split 9–3 for guilty. The second jury in January, 1959, acquitted him. One of the jurors remarked, "You can't send a man to the penitentiary just because he dislikes Jews."

Adolph Rosenberg, the editor of *The Southern Israelite*, remarked that the verdict was expected. "The evidence seemed to rest mostly on circumstances. And, some observers felt, on very little of that."

Insurance covered the cost of rebuilding the Temple. But in addition, hundreds of Christians in Atlanta offered contributions. The Board of Education made one of the schools available for the Temple's religious school, and while repairs were under way, the congregation met in a variety of churches.

What emerged from the bombing of the temple in Atlanta was not estrangement and despair or terror, but security for Jews. Christians in Atlanta were disturbed by the bombing, but more important, they did not feel remote from it.

Atlanta for as long as it has been Atlanta prided itself on its progressive, burgeoning growth. Boosterism, the boast "Watch Us Grow," had its birth not in Sinclair Lewis' Zenith but in the South after the Civil War, and Atlanta was probably its parent. The boosters deplored lynching as soon as they realized the lynchers destroyed not only life but property, too, and they deplored bombings which inhibited growth and commerce.

Additionally, Atlanta is no longer a homogeneous city. It probably has more citizens born in the North among its population than citizens born in the South. It has Lebanese and Greeks. It has a genuine black middle class. It is, in short, a metropolis, and few believe they can preserve the Southern way of life in a city whose airport, one of the largest in the world, accommodates 500 European flights a week.

Lastly, the leaders of Atlanta condemned the bombing as an intolerable moral outrage. They implicated themselves and thus implicated many of their constituents. Leaders become leaders by virtue of their ability to elicit a response from their constituents.

In his monograph on the bombing, Arnold Shankman writes in the November, 1971, issue of the *American Jewish Archives*:

> . . . Atlantans of all faiths learned that, unless they acted, the brotherhood they so long preached would be exposed as meaningless banter. For the city's Jews, remembering that Atlanta had been the site of the Leo M. Frank trial, the response of the community was especially heartening. . . . The Federal authorities, moreover, realized after the bombing that

the FBI should have a role in helping police solve this type of crime, and Congress gave more serious study to proposed legislation to make such deeds violations of Federal law. It is not unlikely that the dynamiting may have influenced some three hundred Atlanta clergymen to sign a statement asking for the preservation of freedom of speech, tolerance for individuals of different races, communication between whites and blacks, and support of those trying to keep schools open."

Why did it happen? Why was this Jewish congregation and not some other chosen as the target? Although no one said so to his face, some members suspected that Rabbi Jacob M. Rothschild had brought this upon them by his outspoken defense of human rights for the black man.

As early as 1948, he had preached to the congregation:

"We must do more than 'view with alarm' the growing race hatred that threatens the South. . . .

"The solution for the ills of the South rests with the people of the South. That much of its claim is valid. . . .

"The problem is ours to solve—and the time for solution is now. We do not have the right to postpone and procrastinate. . . .

"It becomes increasingly obvious that unless decent people take up the burden, the South faces a return to the most primitive kind of bigotry and race hatred."

From that time on, hardly an occasion passed that he did not take the opportunity to speak on this subject. Drop by drop the words began to take effect, so that when the Supreme Court decision on school integration came in 1954, not only the rabbi and a "faithful remnant," but a substantial portion of the congregation made some effort to help implement the decision.

That same year the Temple's president, William Breman, joined Rabbi Rothschild in issuing a plea to all members to vote against a proposed amendment to the Georgia Constitution which would obstruct school integration. The following year both the Couples' Club and the Sisterhood presented programs dealing with civil rights. The Couples' Club sponsored, as its first offering to the congregation, a forum discussion based on a dramatic dialogue dealing with the whole spectrum of man's obligation to his fellowman.

The Sisterhood went a step farther and planned a luncheon meeting entitled "Ourselves and Our Conscience —The Moral and Legal Aspects of Desegregation." Speaking for the legal side was Morris B. Abram, then a resident of Atlanta and member of the congregation. The moral side was represented by the Reverend Dr. Benjamin E. Mays, president of Morehouse College. The subject of the program apparently did not disturb even the more timorous Temple members, but the fact that the distinguished black leader and his wife had been invited to have lunch with the Sisterhood did. To their great credit, Sisterhood leaders refused to succumb to the considerable pressure brought to bear upon them. They proceeded with the luncheon as planned and with notable success. Since then many meetings have been held at the Temple with black guests, both as speakers and as part of the audience.

Meanwhile, Rabbi Rothschild continued to preach on civil rights not only from his pulpit but elsewhere in the city and in the South. In 1956 he told an audience in Jackson, Mississippi, the same thing he had been telling his congregation in Atlanta. The following year from the pulpits of Central Synagogue in New York City and Isaac M. Wise Temple in Cincinnati, he declared, "There is a macabre and disquieting parallel between the South today and a totalitarian state. There is a curtailment of the right to speak freely and openly if what you say disagrees with the popular point of view." What made the words significant was that he had already spoken them in the South.

Rabbi Jacob Rothschild has been a worthy successor to Rabbi Dr. Marx. He was installed as the rabbi of the Temple in 1946 and instituted a series of social action activities.

Rabbi Rothschild's first encounter with the syndrome of Southern Jewry, "Don't dare speak out," came in 1947. The state of Georgia at that time had two men claiming to be its legally designated governor; a group of Atlanta's leading citizens planned a mass meeting to protest the situation. Rabbi Rothschild, along with top clergymen of most Christian denominations, was invited to join this group and unhesitatingly accepted. The names of the participating clergymen appeared in the press the next morning. That evening at an annual meeting of the Temple a member asked to say a few words as to the impropriety of a clergyman becoming involved in politics. Other members of the congregation agreed with the speaker. They did not yet know of the convictions of this young rabbi on social action. It was to be brought home forcibly ten years later on that fatal morning when the Temple was blasted by dynamite.

The Atlanta congregations are:

The Temple, 1589 Peachtree Road, Rabbi Jacob M. Rothschild; Assistant Rabbi Alvin Sugarman.

Ahavath Achim, 600 Peachtree Battle Avenue, NW, Rabbi Dr. Harry H. Epstein; Associate Rabbi David H. Aurbach; Cantor Isaac Goodfriend.

Shearith Israel, 1180 University Drive, NE, Rabbi Donald Friedman; Cantor Sherwood Plitnick.

Or VeShalom, 1681 North Druid Hills Road, NE, Rabbi Robert Ichay; Rabbi Emeritus Joseph Cohen.

Anshe S'Fard, 1324 North Highland Avenue, NE, President Label Merlin; Honorary President and Treasurer H. Taratoo.

Beth Jacob, 1855 LaVista Road, NE, Rabbi Emanuel Feldman, Assistant Rabbi Herbert Cohen; Cantor Benjamin Stiefl.

Temple Sinai, Church of Atonement, 4945 High Point Road, NE, Rabbi Richard Lehrman.

Anti-Semitism has never been as respectable in the United States as it has in Europe. In Europe, Jew baiting is a profession. In America, anti-Semitism is more felt than heard. But it is there, and anyone who is Jewish knows it is there.

Only once in this country has a Jewish community feared for its livelihood and the lives of its members. That fearful instant came in 1915 in Atlanta, Georgia, an instant in American history which involved not only the Jew and anti-Semitism but also the South, the black man, hard times, mob rule, and the mystery of who murdered a pretty girl in the basement of the factory in which she worked.

The murdered girl was Mary Phagan. She met her death on Saturday, April 26, 1913, Confederate Memorial Day— an important day in the South. She had come to the National Pencil Company at noon to collect her pay, which amounted to $1.20 for ten hours' work. She was found the next morning by a night watchman, strangled, her body tossed atop a coal heap. Her pocketbook was missing. She was fourteen years old.

The South cherishes its womanhood. The crime outraged Atlanta. But more was at stake. During the past winter, farmers had burned their cotton as fuel when the price fell below 5 cents a pound. In the previous five years hundreds upon hundreds of farmers had abandoned the countryside to find jobs in the mills near the cities where they worked fourteen hours a day for as little as $11 a week. They labored for absentee landlords, the millowners who lived in Chicago, New York, or San Francisco and only collected profits. That a little girl who made 12 cents an hour putting the rubber eraser into the metal clasp of the pencil would be murdered in such a factory was the last straw.

The newspapers and the public demanded the police arrest her killer. The police arrested every man who had been seen around the factory that afternoon, among them Leo Frank, a Cornell graduate, a Jew from New York, the twenty-nine-year-old production superintendent of the National Pencil Company, a nephew of the owners. He had paid Mary Phagan her wages, making him the last man to see her alive.

Beside Mary Phagan's body, which had not been sexually molested, the police found two handwritten penciled notes which identified her killer as a "long slim Negro." No one for a minute thought Mary Phagan had written these notes. Everyone was sure her killer had written them to throw suspicion from himself. The writer of these notes, the police discovered, was Jim Conley, the black janitor of the factory. But the police were determined to convict Leo Frank, and at his trial Jim Conley swore Leo Frank had dictated the notes to him. Frank commented, "If you found Conley's shirt beside her, you would suspect him. If you found his gun, you would be sure. But you find his handwriting and you insist I killed her."

The question is: Why would the police and the newspapers and all Atlanta want to convict the innocent man and let the guilty man go free? That "why" was best answered thirty years later by Luther Otterbein Bricker, Mary Phagan's minister, in a letter to a friend later published in a religious magazine. Bricker recalled his impression on learning that Mary had been murdered and a black man arrested. He said the black's life was a poor price for the little girl's. "But when the police arrested a Jew," he went on, "and a Yankee Jew at that, all of the inborn prejudices against Jews rose up in a feeling of satisfaction, that here would be a victim worthy to pay for the crime."

A black's life wasn't worth Mary Phagan's life. The black man intruded then and still intrudes across the entire spectrum of Southern society. That intrusion corrupted the South, made it poor, sometimes intolerant, and has often destroyed the urge for justice.

Leo Frank was tried that blistering summer in a courtroom on the first floor of the City Hall Building. The crowd which daily gathered in front of this courthouse blocked traffic. Trolley cars had to inch their way through the people. On another side of the building, a crowd constantly pressed against the open windows, some of them leaning over the sills. Behind the building was a row of storage sheds. Hundreds climbed here to get the best view of all, squatting for six or seven hours while the court was in session because the sun made the tarred roofs too hot to sit.

The mob cheered the points made by the prosecutor and booed the refutations of Frank's lawyers. Their yelling drowned the speeches of the defense. Every time one of Frank's lawyers tried to spare his client the crowd shouted to the jury, "Hang the Jew or we'll hang you." Every morning a black-frocked tent evangelist put his head through the window and boomed to the jury, "The Jew is the synagogue of Satan."

Jim Conley testified that Frank murdered Mary Phagan on the second floor of the National Pencil Company, then, after dictating the notes to Conley, enlisted him to help move the body by elevator to the basement. The prosecutor told the jury that Leo Frank was not only a Northerner, but a Jew whose family owned stocks and bonds in Wall Street. In this frenzy, Atlanta convinced itself that all its problems were created by rich Jews and Northern capitalists. Now, at last, it had one of its tormentors in its hands. Frank was convicted and sentenced to be hanged.

In the beginning, the Jews of Atlanta felt no sympathy for Leo Frank. Jews shun a co-religionist involved in a criminal case as one who has brought shame and possible disaster to the congregation. But after Frank's conviction, when anti-Semitism invaded Georgia in the form of boycotts, violence, and libel, Jews actively began to support Frank's fight for freedom after thousands of leading lawyers in America, including a surprisingly large number in Georgia, publicly demanded a new trial.

This support brought a plague of hatred and vilification upon the Jews and upon Leo Frank. It awakened the venomous prejudices of Tom Watson, once the political boss of Georgia. In his early years, Watson had fought for the rights of the poor farmer in Congress. Now he manipulated these men. He had once been a noted historian, but over the years political disappointments deranged him. The Democrats did not nominate him as they had promised for the Vice Presidency in 1896, and by 1913 Watson was embittered, callous, debt-ridden, and often drunk. He published *Watson's Jeffersonian Magazine* and the *Weekly Jeffersonian* in which he constantly hammered away not only at "Railroads," "Big Money," and "Wall Street," but at the blacks, whom he called "gorillas," and at the Roman Catholic Church whose Pope he always called "Jimmy Cheezy." His anti-Catholic crusade had been so effective that the Georgia legislature passed a bill he demanded conferring the authority on grand juries to investigate Catholic convents.

Watson made no editorial comment about Leo Frank during his trial. But when other newspapers in Georgia, political enemies, asked for a new trial, Watson awakened and struck like a viper. He saw in anti-Semitism the tidal wave he needed to ride back to personal power. For two years, to an excited audience, he hammered away at Leo Frank and the Jews. He kept one theme alive: "Our Little Girl—ours by the Eternal God—has been pursued to a hideous death and bloody grave by the Jew." He not only revived his political fortunes with this campaign, but made money at it, his papers selling as soon as they came on the newsstands. He directed the boycott which made many Jewish businessmen close their doors for good, and he helped inspire the red-necks outside Atlanta to form a vigilante organization calling itself the Knights of Mary Phagan.

Leo Frank petitioned the courts of Georgia and the United States thirteen times. The cost of these appeals was astronomical. Contrary to the prosecutor's charge, Leo Frank came from modest circumstances. He soon exhausted his own, his parents', and his father-in-law's resources. His uncles, the Montag brothers, who owned the National Pencil Company, spent $50,000 in lawyers' fees; Albert D. Lasker, the Jewish advertising man who made orange juice popular, contributed another $150,000. Jewish fraternal organizations added more.

When Frank offered new evidence, Georgia higher courts ruled they could order a new trial only on procedural mistakes. When Frank's lawyers pointed out procedural mistakes, the courts ruled that not having introduced the objections at his trial, Frank could not now offer them.

Frank finally had one last chance—the Supreme Court of the United States—at which point Louis Marshall entered the case, serving without fee. No one in American Jewish life occupied the position Louis Marshall did from 1905 to 1930. No Jew has ever achieved his prominence as a constitutional lawyer with a worldwide reputation (it was Marshall who won the right from the Supreme Court for Oregon Catholics to send their children to parochial schools).

Leonard Roan, Frank's trial judge, was so sure of Frank's innocence that he asked the defense lawyers to keep their client out of the courtroom when the verdict was read lest the mob lynch Frank when they heard "Not guilty." Roan had waived Frank's right to face his jurors. Using this as a constitutional wedge, Marshall opened up the conditions under which Frank had been tried.

Marshall failed. He convinced only two of the Supreme Court judges, Charles Evans Hughes, who later ran for President against Woodrow Wilson, and Oliver Wendell Holmes, the Yankee from Olympus.

"Mob law," wrote Holmes in his dissent, "does not become due process of law by securing the assent of a terrorized jury." This dissent made the Leo Frank case a landmark case, a place along the way where the Supreme Court changed direction. Eight years later, in 1923, Holmes reread his dissent, this time as the majority ruling reversing the conviction of five blacks who had been tried in forty-five minutes by an all-white mob. The Supreme Court quoted

Holmes again in 1963 in reversing another murder conviction.

Cold comfort for Leo Frank, however, whose only hope for life was that the governor of the state would use his powers to commute the sentence from hanging to life imprisonment.

The governor of Georgia was John M. Slaton, who had every expectation of going on to the United States Senate when his term expired in June, 1915, a few weeks away. Tom Watson had promised if Slaton did nothing about the Frank commutation, the nomination was his. But while John Slaton was a rich man, a politician, and a compromiser, ambitious, he was also in his heart of hearts a Christian. He reviewed the trial record, the new evidence, the appeals. And he did more; he became a detective, retracing through the factory step by step the actions the prosecutor had alleged. He convinced himself Leo Frank was innocent, that Jim Conley had murdered Mary Phagan for her pay envelope. If he let Leo Frank hang, he confided to his associates, he would be committing judicial murder.

Slaton's term ended on June 26, 1915. He could have done nothing and let his successor deal with the problem. But he took the case under advisement on June 12, and until he left office, he received daily threats that his home would be burned and he and his wife harmed if he spared the Jew. Commuting Frank's sentence was more than a dangerous judicial option; it was political suicide. Yet he issued the order commuting Frank's sentence on June 21.

When this news spread through Atlanta, crowds began gathering in the hall of the State House of Representatives. Another mob milled in front of the governor's office.

Jewish businessmen closed up early, locked their homes,

and began checking into hotels. Many husbands took their wives and families to the railroad station and sent them to stay with relatives outside the state.

By sundown the mob realized Slaton was not coming to the Capitol. They drifted along the city streets, gaining momentum as workers from the mills joined them. Then the mob crashed into Atlanta's Jewish district in the South Side to find only darkened homes, the streets patrolled by deputy sheriffs. At that moment, the mob became a lynch mob and elected a substitute—John Slaton.

Five thousand angry people, many of them armed with pistols, rifles, saws, and hatchets, marched toward the Buckhead Mansion, where Slaton lived. They surrounded the house, and would not listen to Slaton when he appeared. They would have hanged him then and there, but earlier in the evening the governor's attorney general had called up the Horse Guard, who arrived in time to beat back this mob, many of the guardsmen sustaining serious injuries. It was the only time in American history a governor had to call up the militia to save his own life for an official act.

Six weeks later twenty-five Knights of Mary Phagan stormed the Milledgeville Prison Farm, seized Leo Frank, transported him 175 miles over back roads, and hanged him from an oak tree near the house where Mary Phagan had been born. Leo Frank's agony ended on August 17, 1915, when he was killed by the first lynch party on record in the South to have used automobiles.

Certainly this was not the first lynching in the South. It was, however, one of the first to warn the American people that lynching was not a rural condition to be tolerated but a national problem to be abolished. Lynching still remains an American phenomenon, but now the federal government moves to punish lynchers. Too often Americans think a political decision and a legal distinction are one and the same. Since Americans make laws, they presume wrongly they can unmake them. Since they determine what a judge can do, they presume they can do it themselves.

On Thanksgiving Day of 1915, the Knights of Mary Phagan climbed Stone Mountain, the huge yellow bluff which overlooks Atlanta. They burned a fiery cross at its crest, visible throughout the city, to announce they had rechristened themselves the Reincarnated Invisible Empire of the Knights of the Ku Klux Klan. By the 1920's the Ku Klux Klan numbered in the millions, a vast national organization whose campaign of hatred against black, Catholic, Jew, and foreigner continued unabated. While the Klan never dictated politics on a national level—they could not keep the nomination for President from Alfred E. Smith, a Roman Catholic governor of New York—on the local level in the South and in Indiana, Illinois, and New Jersey, the Klan was all-powerful. Everyone from sheriff to dog catcher was a Klansman, parading every Sunday down Main Street carrying blackjacks and whips, dressed in white bedsheets with hoods covering their faces, two round holes for the eyes.

Half the 3,000 Jews in Georgia left the state after the lynching. John M. Slaton, whose car was pursued by red-necks shouting, "Slaton, Slaton, King of the Jews!" also left Georgia on the day his term ended and did not return for six years. Tom Watson went to the Senate, where he died in office in 1922.

When a Georgia Congressman suggested in the 1950's that the Post Office issue a stamp to honor Tom Watson as the father of rural free delivery, the Postmaster General ruled Watson was not well known enough. In 1957 the

Georgia legislature authorized the John M. Slaton Memorial. Slaton's bust graces the State Capitol over the inscription "The Incomparable Georgian."

The Jewish Stereotype

THE JEWS who came back to Atlanta and who migrated to other cities in the South worked assiduously at assimilation. They were at pains to keep a "low profile." They and the power structure of the South were always at pains to agree there was no anti-Jewish prejudices. The ability to deny the virulence has always been a Southern characteristic. During these decades, the white power structure was also proclaiming that the way to end lynchings was for blacks to behave themselves.

The milieu enforced differences between Jews in the North and the South. In 1867, Atlanta Jews founded the synagogue Gamilath, Chesed, or Hebrew Benevolent Congregation. For fifty years, between 1895 and 1945 its rabbi was David Marx, one of the first American-born rabbis to hold a pulpit in the South. Rabbi Marx accompanied Lucille Frank on the train when she brought the coffin which contained the corpse of her husband, Leo, home to Brooklyn for burial.

As the spiritual leader of this Reform temple Rabbi Marx did not confer Bar Mitzvah, even upon request. He urged his congregants to ignore the dietary laws. He held Sunday services for those unable to attend on the Sabbath eve. But he remained the spiritual conscience of Atlanta Jewry for all the years of his rabbinate.

In Richmond, Rabbi Edward Nathan Calisch of Beth

Ahabah became one of the founders of the Central Conference of American Rabbis who, from the time of the Balfour Declaration, opposed the concept of Palestine as *the* homeland of Jews. Such a concept, argued Calisch, diminished the integrity of the American Jew as a citizen and compromised his patriotism. The Jewish mission he went on was a universal mission to infuse the world with values, not a mission to insure the survival of a race.

In Northern cities like Cleveland, Rabbi Abba Hillel Silver and Barnett Brickner worked unceasingly to lead the Jews into a love for Zion. Louis D. Brandeis had insisted that to be good Americans, Jews had to become good Jews, and to become good Jews, they owed an emotional allegiance to a Jewish homeland. In New York Rabbi Stephen Wise recruited the support of Episcopal and Catholic bishops for an Israel.

So persuasive were the rabbis of the North that by 1944 the formation of a Jewish state was one of the planks included by both the Republican and Democratic parties. But a man has to think long and hard before remembering a Zionist spokesman in the South.

Let us remember, however, not only that conformity is the chief civil virtue of the South but that the South and Southerners considered themselves remote, isolated, and removed from the tumult of the industrial city. The menace Hitler posed was somehow to be blunted by the Mason-Dixon Line and the Smokies. And it is true that Jews the world over came late to the realization of the Nazi extermination.

Jewish leadership in the South thought it could hide in the tall corn. I like often to tell the story of the impassioned telephone call I received from the editor of the Charlotte *News* one night in 1948. "Harry," said the editor, urgently, "we ran a headline that said, 'Arabs Down Two Jew Planes,' and the switchboard is lit up like a menorah. What did we do wrong?"

"It's a long story," I replied. "Change the 'Jew' to 'Israeli' for the bulldog edition. Someday, when I get time to write a book, I'll explain it to you."

On the occasion of Israel's first anniversary in 1949, Governor Olin Johnston of South Carolina stood before a Jewish audience and quoted from Ezekiel how God gave the Holy Land to the Jews. Lowering his voice, the governor said, "Of course, now that Israel has become a state, I shall be sorry to see many of my friends leaving South Carolina."

The Jewish businessmen down there are still shaking.

The Jews of the South had done such an ineffective job of educating their neighbors about what precisely Jews believed that in the 1950's when Governor Ross Barnett of Mississippi presided over the founding of a new temple, he addressed the congregants as "fellow Christians." When his error was pointed out to him by the rabbi and the New York *Times*, Ross said, "Why, Ah thought we were all neighbors, down he-ah."

The assimilation Southern Jews desired was not to be. The power structure accepted them as neighbors, but the red-necks did not. In November, 1957, congregants accidentally and fortunately found eleven sticks of dynamite in Charlotte's Temple Beth-El. In the next few months bombs were found in synagogues in Gastonia, North Carolina, and in Birmingham, Alabama. A bomb did indeed go off in a Miami synagogue, and the next day a bomb exploded at the Nashville Jewish Community Center. A little later another damaged the Jacksonville Community Center.

In each of these instances, the bombers forewarned their

victims. The bombers had chosen the Jews as victims, they said, because the Jews had declared war on the human race by preaching integration, though as a matter of fact the Jews in these cities were preaching anything but.

Racial Segregation and Rabbi Mantinband

THE STEREOTYPE dogged the Jews of the South more persistently than the Jews of the North. There were, after all, stereotypes in the North, but there were very few in the South.

When the nine Justices of the Supreme Court ruled that segregation of the schools was unconstitutional, no Baptist, Presbyterian, or Methodist felt threatened because there were Baptists, Presbyterians, and Methodists on the Supreme Court. But the Jews felt threatened because Felix Frankfurter sat on the high bench.

When Bishop Oxnam championed the cause of black equity in New York, no one charged that Methodists were trying to mongrelize the race. When Jack Greenfield of the Legal Defense Fund of the National Association for the Advancement of Colored People went to court on behalf of James Meredith, Southerners charged all Jews were conspiring.

Desegregation split the Jews of the South as it split the Jews of the country, in fact as it split the whole of the United States.

One of the most effective of the segregationists was Charles J. Bloch of Macon, elected "Man of the Year" by the Georgia County Commissioners Association in 1958, no light honor.

Bloch, a native of Baton Rouge, Louisiana, came to Macon as a young boy in 1901. He was graduated from the University of Georgia and from Mercer University Law School, after which he joined the Southern Railroad, whose chief counsel he now is. The Southern includes the Alabama Great Southern, Albany Northern, Georgia Northern, and my favorite, the Georgia, Ashburn, Sylvester and Camilia.

Charles Bloch nominated Richard Russell of Georgia at the 1948 Democratic Convention and then led the Georgia delegation out when the Truman faction forced a vote on a civil rights plank.

What endeared Charles Bloch to the county commissioners was his authorship of *States Rights—The Law of the Land* which established Mr. Bloch as an authority of the Constitution of the United States (a great many legal treatises which argued that the Constitution says white kids don't have to go to school with black kids established their authors as constitutional authorities).

Mr. Bloch also resuscitated "interposition" and "nullification" as legal ploys to thwart federal attempts to force school integration. But this inventiveness was discouraged by federal judges.

I have little sympathy for Mr. Bloch's legal certainties, but I am sure his motives are genuine. Nonetheless, all his efforts and ingenuity did not influence a Georgia editor who wrote in 1960, "The Jews are trying to mongrelize the South."

Charles Mantinband, the rabbi of B'nai Israel in Hattiesburg, Mississippi, a Virginia boy who has held pulpits in several cities of the deep South, has been known as a mischief-maker. From his pulpit and as spokesman for a

93

variety of liberal causes, he has publicly and continuously deplored racial segregation.

Mantinband, who rather resembles the late A. J. Liebling, is noted as a poet and wit in these endeavors. He is the author of "Come weal, come woe/ My status is quo," which is the anthem of a large majority of Southern Jewry. When he joined a clergyman's group in Hattiesburg, a minister asked, "How shall I address you, Rabbi? I call my other colleagues Brother Hones, Brother Smith, and Brother Robinson."

"Call me Brother-in-Law," replied Mantinband.

When blacks entered his home, a neighbor demanded, "Rabbi, who are those people?"

"Some of my Christian friends," said Mantinband.

When a national foundation contributed $2,500 to the Hattiesburg temple in honor of what it deemed Mantinband's sane approach and wisdom in dealing with the race issue, B'nai Israel's board was panicky and hesitant about accepting the money. Its members were afraid of reprisals. B'nai Israel accepted the money after Mantinband made it clear that if it were refused not only would the temple lose this income but its rabbi as well.

The difference between these two Jews, Charles Bloch and Charles Mantinband, pales when one considers the enormity of the racial problem. It is obviously a world problem whose bitterness and complexity almost overwhelm us.

We Jews of the South who thought humor, reason, logic and humanity would resolve this problem were simply wrong because we failed to sense how deeply imbued race and the distinction between men are. Those Jews who thought it was wisest to perpetuate the "Southern way of life," however, were simply crazy.

Religion, Mixed Marriage, and Fears Among the Jews of the South

THIRTY-THREE YEARS AGO, I got off a train in Charlotte, North Carolina. From the train station I could see the Charlotte Hotel (still standing), the Greyhound Bus Terminal, the Post Office, and the Oriental Restaurant. Charlotte wasn't 100,000 then; now it is a city of almost 300,000.

I was in the vanguard of a vast migration that has changed the face of America. The farmers and the rural poor began migrating to the cities before the turn of the century. By 1932 there were more people in the cities than in the countryside.

Then people began to shake out of the cities in the Northeast and Midwest. The fabulous growth of Los Angeles which began after World War II is one example of this change. Probably as many immigrants have come into the industrialized cities of the South as have ventured to the Pacific.

Among them are 540,000 Jews from Miami to Dallas to Baltimore. They were part of a migration which was not Jewish. For the Jews who came to America came together, although they came in four different waves. And as they moved into cities, they moved together.

But that is not how Jews moved into the South, with the exception of the Savannah accession in 1733. This experience doesn't make them a different kind of Jew, but it has made their life in the South appreciably different.

Among the thousands of Cuban refugees who came to Miami after Castro's revolution were several Jews, the children of European Jews who fled Hitler in the 1930's.

Another cohort of Jews settled in the Dominican Republic.

One of them, Diego Grynspan, settled for a while in Charlotte, and I will wager another forty settled between Jacksonville and Richmond. They got into the franchises. They ran the Hertz or Avis or Taylor Supply or Carvel outlets, like most Jews performing an actuarial role.

Many Jews come to the large Southern cities with the malls and the shopping centers. Many come as chemists or physicists or engineers in the scientific complex of industry. Jews in the South now work in state, federal, and municipal government.

But the major worry of the Jews in the South, particularly in the smaller towns, is that more Jews leave than come. Savannah, for example, once had a population of 5,000 Jews; now it has 2,900. Charleston, West Virginia, is barely 1,100 Jews where once it was 2,500. The problem is that these communities are slowly becoming communities of the elderly.

In short, the young do not want to go into the family store. There are Jewish stores by the score throughout the South managed by the May chain or J. C. Penney because there were no successors to the original merchant. The young Jewish doctor will pick a city congenial to his professional and private interests. The accountant will work for a conglomerate, aiming always to succeed to the headquarters as a comptroller.

The South leads the country in the number of congregations in proportion to the number of Jewish residents, with one congregation for every 600 Jews. The national average is one congregation for every 1,300 Jews. There are several reasons for this. In the first place, there is the natural inclination to conform to the habits of the surrounding

Rabbi Gershon Mendes Seixas, famous rabbi and member of the board of trustees of Columbia University. 1745–1816.

David Lopez. 1750–1816.

Photographs courtesy of American Jewish Archives

Thomas Kennedy won religious freedom for the Jews in Maryland. 1776–1832.

Judah Touro contributed $10,000 toward the building of the Bunker Hill Monument. 1775–1854.

Isaac Harby, journalist and literary critic, founder
of the Jewish Reform movement. Born 1788.

Jacob Mordecai, founder of the first private school
for girls in the South, father of Alfred
and M. C. Mordecai.

Alfred Mordecai, soldier, teacher,
scientist. 1802–1887.

M. C. Mordecai. 1804–1888.

Rabbi David Einhorn, the abolitionist rabbi of Baltimore. Born 1809.

Isaac Leeser, famous journalist and civic leader, founded Hebrew College. 1806–1868.

David Levy Yulee, first Jewish member
of the United States Senate. Born 1810.

Judah P. Benjamin, Senator, "the brains
of the Confederacy." 1811–1884.

Edwin de Leon.

David Camden de Leon,
Surgeon General of the
Confederate Army. 1814–
1872.

society, and the South is the most "church-minded" section in the country. There are, of course, many pious Jews to whom the synagogue is a necessary part of everyday living, but their proportion is no greater than the national average. The difference is explained, at least partly, by this intense religiosity of the Christian majority, and the Jews, of all people, are *expected* to be members of a religious organization.

Their economic status is certainly a weighty factor in the ability of Jews to build and maintain religious establishments. It is reflected, too, in the per capita contribution to the United Jewish Appeal, which, according to official statistics, runs as much as 20 percent above the national average. The number of contributions in proportion to the population is even greater. It is much easier to contact every individual prospect; his business, social, and philanthropic activities are an open book, and the desire to maintain status is another stimulus to maximum giving. There are Southern cities of 200 Jewish families with 195 individual pledges. While essentially the giving is motivated by a deep sense of responsibility for the survivors of Hitler's massacre, as well as an almost unanimous devotion to the ideal that is Israel, it is also a fact that the mechanics of organized Jewish philanthropy in the South are more conducive to maximum gifts and a greater proportion of contributors. The higher average of giving and greater proportion of contributors extend also the campaigns within the general community—Community Chest, Red Cross, and hospital drives. There are schools, playgrounds, hospitals, and Christian churches throughout the South which bear the imprint of Jewish generosity.

There is yet another major reason for the seemingly closer religious life of the Jew in the South. The temple is in fact the alpha and omega of all Jewish communal life. The attendance at the religious services, Orthodox, Conservative, and Reform, is not one iota greater than the attendance at religious services elsewhere, but the attendance in the recreational hall and banquet room is far beyond that of the other Jewish communities. The temple is the center of all "defense," social, philanthropic, and cultural activities. The social segregation between the Jew and non-Jew intensifies this. Consider, too, that the outside entertainment and cultural activities are rarer than in the Northern metropolitan centers.

Still, it would not be fair to say that the bazaars put on by the temple sisterhoods and the card games sponsored by the temple brotherhoods draw capacity crowds, without noting that a lecture by a Rabbi Mordecai Kaplan will bring out the entire Jewish community as well.

In this matter of temple affiliation it is interesting to watch the reaction of the newcomer to the community (now an everyday occurrence). In his first contacts with the local Jewish community he is asked to join the temple. His answer has become a standing joke, because he generally will say one of two things: "I am an agnostic and do not believe in that stuff," or "I never go to *shul* more than once, maybe twice a year." The local residents smile knowingly, and there the matter rests. A month later Mr. Newcomer is pulling wires to become a director of the temple, and his wife is knee-deep in rummage sales with the ladies of the auxiliary.

About one out of every three Jewish boys takes a Christian wife. The percentage is only slightly lower in the larger cities. Propinquity and biology are the only motivating factors. Incidentally, the mixed marriages are consistent with the social segregation which exists between Jew and non-Jew. The Jew must always bring to the union something more than himself; the social cleavage is bridged by the special advantages the Jew contributes to the marriage. He will marry the Gentile girl who works in his father's store; he'll not marry the Gentile daughter of his father's competitor. Despite the higher economic level to which she usually ascends, the Christian girl presumably makes the greater sacrifice. She finds herself constantly justifying her marriage to a Jew. In effect she says to others and to herself: "He's a Jew, but he's rich," "He's a Jew, but he's a writer . . . college professor, etc." Invariably, the Jewish male involved in intermarriage is a man who is self-sustaining by career. Rarely does a Jewish taxi driver marry a Christian.

These mixed marriages have become so commonplace that they do not cause a ripple within the Jewish community; on the other hand, a Jew with a Christian wife does not change the status of his application for membership in the Gentile country club or automatically qualify his children for the exclusive private school.

One Jewish merchant had the right idea about this intermarriage. He was a man with four stores in four different cities of North Carolina. He also had four daughters, and he wrote a letter to all his suppliers: "If you want to sell me goods, send me a salesman with the following qualifications: He must be Jewish, and he must be single." That's precisely how it happened. All the four daughters were married to these salesmen, and each of them is operating one of the stores that their father left them, and they are raising fine families.

It is well to note that in recent years there have been a considerable number of converts to Judaism. In these cases the non-Jewish wife enters upon her duties in maintaining a

Jewish home with an ardor seldom seen in the Jewish community itself. In one town, a converted wife asked her husband why he insisted upon maintaining a kosher home and why he objected to a Christmas tree "when your own two sisters don't keep kosher and also have a Christmas tree every year." Indeed hers was the only kosher home in town.

When the Christian wife does not enter in the Jewish faith (and the great majority of course do not), they each maintain separate religious affiliations. Many practicing Christian wives attend Friday night and High Holiday services with their husbands. Some of them teach in the Sunday schools of their own churches. In the recent organization of a new temple in North Carolina, four of the eight charter members had Christian wives.

The Jews of the Southern communities live in deadly fear of a disturber. This fear has nothing whatever to do with current political tensions. The studied attempt to avoid all debate, except on purely Jewish matters, has been in force so long that it would be hard to find six Jews below the Mason-Dixon Line who hold sufficiently strong convictions to be accused of anything. When the Hebrew Union College sent word that the term "Reform Judaism" had been officially changed to "Liberal Judaism," the directors of one temple challenged the idea. They reasoned that the word "liberal" had no place in religion. Through the fear of all is that the agitator be a "pink," a worker for a black cause. In a rally for the Scottsboro boys a few years ago by two Protestant clergymen, not a single Jew made an appearance.

Let us note, however, that though their number is small, there are liberal, politically aware, and socially conscious Jews in every Southern community. Paradoxically these Jewish nonconformists are far less exclusive than those who try so desperately to hew the line. These one or two Jewish liberals in each town find natural allies among the Gentile nonconformists, dissenters, Unitarians, and humanists. They weld themselves into an even smaller minority and pursue all their political, cultural, and social activities together.

The basic truth is that in general the Jew is distrusted by the low-income group and disliked by the middle class, and he is powerless to affect the course of this phobia even to the slightest degree. Yet vocal anti-Semitism is much less evident in the South than in Massachusetts or New York. To a great extent the deep concern of the Southerner over "the Negro" serves as a shock absorber for the Jewish minority. In addition, the South has in recent years produced many influential liberals, particularly among the Protestant clergy and the editors and publishers of the daily press. With resurgence of small Ku Klux Klan elements, three clergymen in one city attacked the hoodlums from their pulpits, unthinkable twenty-five or thirty years ago. The Methodist-Episcopal Church South (now part of the main Methodist Fellowship) was the first major non-Jewish organization in the world officially to condemn Hitler's racial laws (1934).

Primarily the Jews of the South reflect to a large extent the mores, the hopes, the politics, and even the prejudices of the society around them. The pattern follows an instinctive search for the security which comes with some degree of anonymity. Nothing reflects this desire more poignantly than the all too common boast that "My son looks like a Georgia cracker" (or a "Tarheel" or a "Tennessee mountaineer").

The observation that *m'ken leben ober m'lust nisht* (you can live but they won't let you) can be tragic at times, but more often it is humorous. Recently, a wealthy old-timer with a long and honorable record of good works and philanthropies in his community, was appointed to an important secular board in the Christian community when it was making preparations for a fund-raising drive for a new hospital building. He was the first Jew ever to achieve this distinction. It was a great honor. As he left after attending his first session, he had a look of chagrin on his face, and with the air of a man both sad and tired he said, "The *mommzer* gave me all the Jewish cards. . . ."

Family and the South

"THE FAMILY" GATHERS for Thanksgiving or for the Seder meal. "Family," the word without the article, denotes pedigree.

In Europe, royalty was the pedigree.

In America, in the beginning, which was not so long ago, the pedigree was money or longevity.

The Jews of the South usually had neither.

Those Americans in the North, in the flush of post-Civil War affluence, set about establishing "family" by collecting royalty much as archaeologists set about collecting artifacts.

They collected not only royalty, but the portraits of earlier royalty, and not only the portraits, but the very walls from which the portraits hung. When millionaires couldn't collect the castles, and shipping them stone by stone across the Atlantic was impossible, they copied them. Americans gave up this quest for a variety of reasons, chief of which is that unemployed royalty is usually talentless and we are a practical people.

The more sentimental Southerners, in the wretchedness of post-Civil War poverty, established pedigree by longevity. Determining who was and who was not "family" fed genealogists for several decades. Money was not a crucial instrument in this determination. Indeed, many a DAR member has borrowed the bus fare to attend the national convention in Washington, D.C.

Pedigree in the modern world descends through power and influence. Money and longevity are still important, but more important is a family's ability to publicize itself, to attract attention, to generate fame. William Henry and his grandson, Benjamin, were one of three sets of "tandem" Presidents, but no commentator has ever invested the Harrisons with the romance untold commentators have invested in the Kennedys, the brothers of whom were almost tandem Presidents.

Jews have entered the hagiography of "family" in the Eastern Establishment, but not in the Southern for the simple reason the Southern Establishment cannot boast power and influence. One establishes "family" in a stable society. For a longer period of its history, the South was a frontier rather than a society. J. W. Cash, in *The Mind of the South*, remarked that young men who cleared the Carolinas and Tennessee of Indians lived to command battalions at Bull Run. Not only is it hard for a "family" to survive on the frontier, but it is hard to survive.

It is true there was an antebellum society in the South. That society was a plantation society, its crop, cotton. Cotton did not become a profitable export until the invention of the cotton gin which Eli Whitney and Phineas Miller began to manufacture in 1794. The cotton gin made the Southern plantation society a possibility. It was a late start. By 1794 John Adams knew that in two years he would become the second President of the United States, and his son, John Quincy, embarking on a political career was hoping he might be a President, too.

The Civil War broke the South in two. For twelve years of its history, 1865 to 1877, it was an occupied nation. Until Buck Duke built the first power plant on the Catawba River in North Carolina in 1906, the South was hopelessly broke. For a long time thereafter it remained broke, but not hopelessly. Poor people do not wield power and influence. Lyndon Johnson from Texas was the first Southerner elected President by the national constituency since Zachary Taylor took office in 1849.

It is little wonder the South was producing Strauses, Warburgs, or Lehmans. It was not producing Du Ponts, Rockefellers, or Roosevelts.

The Cause

AT THE BEGINNING of the Civil War, there were 150,000 Jews in the United States, a preponderance of them immigrants from Germany. Seven thousand Jews fought for the Union, and 1,500 for the Confederacy. Nothing in their Judaism convinced Jews of the South that slavery was a moral horror, and nothing in *their* Judaism convinced Jews of the North that internecine war was a catastrophe.

Twenty years before, Alexis de Tocqueville in Volume II of *Democracy in America* remarked:

> The American ministers of the Gospel do not attempt to draw or fix all the thoughts of man upon the life to come; they are willing to surrender a portion of his heart to the cares of the present, seeming to consider the goods of this world as

important, though secondary objects. If they take no part themselves in productive labor, they are at least interested in its progress and they applaud its results; and while they never cease to point to the other world as the great object of the hopes and fears of the believer, they do not forbid him honestly to court prosperity in this. Far from attempting to show that these things are distinct and contrary to one another, they study rather to find out on what point they are most nearly and closely connected.

While Rabbi David Einhorn of Baltimore was so fiery an abolitionist that his congregation chased him from his pulpit, Rabbi Maximillian Michelbacher of Richmond circulated a prayer for Jewish soldiers in Confederate ranks which began "Our firesides are threatened, the foe is before us."

The Civil War transformed the Northern butcher into a meat-packer and the tailor into a manufacturer of uniforms and the sutler into a merchandising tycoon. The Civil War made some Union Jews wealthy men.

While the South was a rural and plantation economy, it had by 1861 a fair degree of industrialization. It was not industrial enough to wage modern war successfully. All of the South's industry was devoted to weaponry and matériel. The Confederate Cabinet had to decide toward the end of the war whether to melt down its surviving locomotive engines to produce cannons. It took two years' salary for a Confederate officer to pay for his uniform. Those Jews of the Confederacy allied with industry, the storekeepers, or the brokers were not ruined by the war—along with the entire mercantile class of the South and the plantation owners they were devastated.

That is probably the singular reason that the South never produced an "Our Crowd."

The Civil War made the Union an industrial world giant. It spurred railroads, the telegraph, manufacturing techniques, shipbuilding and the rest. In the South, sooner or later, every able-bodied man and even the infirm, the elderly, and the children marched to battle.

There were 193 Jewish periodicals in the United States in 1973, some of which predate the Civil War. But there wasn't one in the antebellum South. Three Jews, named Bondi, Wiener, and Benjamin, joined John Brown's raiders in Kansas. They chose to entrust their motives to neither newspapers or diaries. Since the three were storekeepers, we can only presume they joined with John Brown "to cause the Border Ruffians a restraining fear," as Brown himself put it.

Whether the Jews of the South were unselfconscious as Jews is a question I will not hazard. But Southerners themselves were never noted as diarists. W. J. Cash noted in his classic *The Mind of the South*: "In general, the intellectual and aesthetic culture of the old South was a superficial and jejune thing, borrowed from without and worn as a political armor and badge of rank; and hence (I call the authority of old Matthew Arnold to bear me witness) not a true culture at all."

I think for this reason the most articulate sons of the South from William Faulkner to James McBride Dabbs have always described the land as a myth. People who live in a myth are Cavaliers or beauties in crinoline, and there is no reason to suppose the Jews weren't caught up in it, too.

On more than one unfortunate occasion, I have watched television try to integrate the stereotype of the bearded, yarmulke-wearing Talmudic Jew into the myth of the Old South or the Pioneer West with what can only be called less than dramatic results. There were no pushcarts in the Old

South because the heat would spoil produce and no pushcarts in the Pioneer West because the distances were too vast.

What there was in the Civil War South was anti-Semitism, all of it detailed by Rabbi Bertram Korn in his book *Jews in the Civil War*. There was, however, never an actual assault on any Jew, although several grand juries in the South issued blanket condemnations of Jewish hoarding, black marketeering, and speculating. One of these rhetorical indictments so dismayed Lazarus Straus, that he left Talbotton, Georgia, for Columbus, resolving that at the end of the war he would migrate North, which indeed he did, eventually to develop with his sons the great R. H. Macy's department store.

The Jews and Slavery

THE JEWS of the South in general related to slavery as did all other white Americans. Jews were both proslavery and antislavery. There were Jewish slaveholders and Jewish abolitionists, there were Negrophobes and Negrophiles, and Bertram W. Korn, a scholar specializing in American Jewish history, has written that although "Jews in the South were not among slave-holders they participated in every exploitation of the defenseless blacks." This included purchasing, owning, and selling slaves. It included apprehending runaways and meting out punishment. Both in their thinking about and behavior toward slaves, Jews were indistinguishable from their Southern Gentile neighbors.

In the early Federal era, Abraham M. Seixas, a Jewish businessman whose merchandise included slaves, was living in Charleston. Apparently he had a penchant for inserting poetic advertisements in newspapers such as the one which was published by the *South Carolina State Gazette* in 1794:

> Abraham Seixas
> All so gracious
> Once again does offer
> His services pure
> For to secure
> Money in the coffer
> He has for sale
> Some negroes, male,
> Will suit full well grooms
> He has likewise
> Some of their wives
> Can man clean dirty rooms?

Why did Southern Jews, in the main, acquiesce in the *status quo ante bellum?* How can one explain Jewish compliance with and involvement in the slave system?

Bertram Korn has contended that although Jews were few in number and vulnerable to the wrath of the larger community, it was not the specter of anti-Semitism that militated against a distinctively antislavery position. Instead, Korn has pointed to the need of Jewish Americans to be accepted as equals by their neighbors. By copying the example set by Gentile slave masters, they would achieve a psychological and social parity. Thus their accommodation to a new and potentially uncomfortable milieu was accomplished at the expense of the black man.

Race consciousness in Dixie resulted in benefit to the Jew as a white man. Differences between whites were submerged in a society that was preoccupied with maintaining the subordinate status of blacks. In this vein Korn has analyzed the loftier political and social status enjoyed by

Southern Jews than by their Northern co-religionists: "The Negroes acted as an escape valve in Southern society. The Jews gained in status and security from the very presence of this large mass of defenseless victims who were compelled to absorb all of the prejudices which might otherwise have been expressed more frequently in anti-Jewish sentiment."

The Radical—David Einhorn

DAVID EINHORN was born in 1809 in the small Bavarian village of Dipsek, near Fürth. Early in his life he became a student at the famous yeshiva in Würzburg, where he studied under the renowned scholar Wolf Hamburger. Upon ordination, the seventeen-year-old Einhorn did not immediately become a rabbi. He exchanged the hard bench of the yeshiva for that of the university and attended institutions of higher learning in Erlangen, Würzburg, and Munich. He openly expressed his liberal views on religion and rituals and was blocked from securing a post as rabbi by the Bavarian Orthodox leaders. It was only in 1842, at the age of thirty-three, that Einhorn acquired a position and an important one at that. He became chief rabbi in Birkenfeld, in the liberal grand duchy of Oldenburg.

The 1840's were years of great religious controversy among Jews in Germany. Einhorn participated in rabbinical conferences in which his position on all issues was extremely radical. In 1852 he was invited to become rabbi of the Reform congregation in Pest (later part of Budapest). He had served there only two months when the government, feeling that this firebrand might prove dangerous, closed the temple altogether. Einhorn took to writing, and two years later he published his first book, *The Principles of Mosaic Faith and Its Relationship to Paganism and Rabbinic Judaism.* In 1855 Einhorn received the call from Har Sinai Congregation in Baltimore. He was a man of forty-six, a man with a great reputation, when he decided to come to the New World.

In Baltimore, Einhorn found himself rabbi of a small and struggling congregation. On September 27, 1855, he delivered his inaugural sermon. It was much more than just a conventional religious discourse. It was an exposition of a philosophy, a platform of principles, and a call to action. He spoke of the "indisputable fact" that "the old world is fast crumbling to pieces, and a new world seeks to rise from the ruins. . . . Judaism has reached the turning point, which demands the abolition of all defunct usages." Those opposed to slavery had their spokesman in Rabbi Einhorn. In his *Sinai* he denounced slavery as "the cancer of the union." "Does the Negro have an iron neck that does not feel a burdensome yoke? Does he have a stiffer heart that does not bleed when . . . his beloved child is torn away from him?"

Einhorn published four articles in answer to Rabbi Morris Jacob Raphall, who had preached in defense of slavery. In bitterness and pain Einhorn wrote: "A Jew, sapling of that stem, which praises the Lord daily for deliverance out of the Egyptian yoke of slavery, undertook to defend slavery. . . . Woe to the ears that hear such things. . . . We are obliged to reject such words because they are profanation of God's name."

He expected more of Jews than of others. He expected them always to "remember Egypt," and he was shocked to hear that "there are even immigrant Jews, who are so blinded as to be enthusiastic for secession and slavery."

The words of a rabbi carried great weight, not only among Jews, but also in the community at large. The sermons of both Raphall and Einhorn were published and distributed by those who favored their opposing views. Raphall's sermon was quite popular in the South, while one of Einhorn's patriotic sermons was disseminated in the North, the profits from its sale going to the Sanitary Commission.

Einhorn was relentless in calling upon the Jews to take an active part in the Civil War. He considered it the duty of "Israel, the people of peoples . . . to fight *against* the whole world for the whole world," and in this respect he saw no difference between the Jews and the United States as a whole. Like the Jews, this country, too, had a mission. "America of the future will not rest on slave chains, or belittling its adopted citizens. It will also give up its disinterestedness in the fate of other peoples of the world."

This was all published by Einhorn in Baltimore, which, on the whole, was sympathetic to the South. No wonder that many Jews became concerned lest the rabbi's pronouncements endanger their position. A protest meeting of Jews was called in order to make it clear to the general community that this rabbi was speaking only for himself and did not represent the Jewish community.

Einhorn was accused of showing no concern for his fellow Jews. His reply was that on the contrary, he had always been aware that "our entire community is held responsible for the crime of one of us." It was precisely this awareness that obliged him to call upon Jews to "behave decently, to fight against prejudice." He even felt it to be a service to Jews to expose without pity Jewish smugglers. In his *War with Amalek* he called upon American Jews "to make war also upon the Amalek in our own midst . . . who brings shame and disgrace upon our religion."

On April 19, 1861, Federal troops on their way to Washington were attacked by a Baltimore mob. Among those arrested for "assault" was Joseph Friedenwald, son of Jonas Friedenwald. On the following day the printing shops of both abolitionist publications, *Der Wecker* and *Sinai*, were demolished by the mobs. Einhorn's life was in danger, and upon the insistence of the congregation he left the city with his family on May 12. He settled in Philadelphia, where he renewed the publication of *Sinai*. In the first issue he gave a full account of the events that had led to his flight. The magazine continued in Philadelphia for only one year. In the last issue, Einhorn wrote "*Sinai* dies in the battle against slavery."

It is obvious that Einhorn could not have continued as rabbi as long as he did—six full years—if he had not had many supporters in his congregation. After he went to Philadelphia, those who had sided with him wanted him to return to Baltimore. But even while agreeing with the rabbi, they were much more cautious than their leader; in their letter to him they wrote that "for the sake of your own safety as well as out of consideration for the members of your congregation" they were asking him "not to comment from the pulpit on the excitable issues of the time."

How little did his followers know their rabbi if they could suggest to him that he speak only on "Judaism." He naturally rejected this invitation. A committee then went to Philadelphia to prove to him that it was only due to "sad circumstances" that they had asked him not to preach on social issues. To one of his staunchest supporters, Reuben Oppenheimer, he wrote in bitterness on August 12, 1861:

"There is nothing so loathsome, indeed, than this riffraff of bacon reformers. The light of the Rabbis becomes a destroying torch in the hands of such people."

John Brown's Raiders

THREE JEWS RODE with John Brown. Their names were Wiener, Bondi, and Benjamin. Wiener and Benjamin were storekeepers of St. Louis. They had come to Pottawatomie, Kansas, to open a shop together. Bondi had come to Kansas as an agent of Benjamin, to scout around for sites and prospects for the new shops. In September, 1855, they opened the new store and commenced doing business.

Border Ruffians, encouraged by proslavery militants, were trying to extend slavery into Kansas and keep out the abolitionists. They threatened to destroy the shop of Wiener and Benjamin and drive them out of the state—or worse. Wiener and Benjamin, along with Bondi, came with their troubles to the doorstep of John Brown. On May 21, 1856, the Ruffians formed a posse and moved in on Lawrence. There was a good deal of noise, more rowdyism than anything else, and burning and destruction. Yet when the smoke cleared, several abolitionists lay dead, and many others had been arrested for "treason."

This incident triggered some sort of dangerous mechanism inside John Brown. On the night of May 24 he and seven volunteers, including Wiener, crossed Pottawatomie Creek and exacted vengeance on proslavery settlers and Ruffians who lived in the cabins and homes along the creek. Five proslavers lay dead before dawn, the work of Brown and his followers.

In June, Bondi and Wiener fought by John Brown's side in and around Prairie City. Fought the Border Ruffians and captured twenty-six, along with arms and ammunition.

In August, Brown and his men fought back for the savage attack made by the Ruffians on the town of Osawatomie. Bondi and Benjamin were along. Fifty of the enemy were wounded.

John Brown left Kansas, and Wiener went with him. Later, all three of Brown's Jewish comrades enlisted in the Civil War and survived to settle in other states.

A True Confederate Rabbi

JAMES GUTHEIM WAS an immigrant to New Orleans, born in Westphalia, Germany.

In 1846 he became rabbi of Congregation B'nai Jeshurun in Cincinnati. In 1849 he was called to the Shaare Chesed congregation in New Orleans, which he left in 1853 to become rabbi of the Nefutzoth Yehudah congregation in the same city. As he was one of the few rabbis who then preached in English, he was in wide demand as a guest speaker. He was an ardent adherent of the Confederacy, and in 1862, when New Orleans was captured by the Union troops, he closed the doors of his synagogue and for the next two years served as rabbi at Montgomery, Alabama, and Columbus, Georgia. He then returned to New Orleans, but in 1868 accepted a call to Temple Emanu-El of New York City as English preacher. Four years later he returned to New Orleans as minister of the newly founded Reform Jewish congregation, Temple Sinai, this being the third congregation in that city in which he officiated. He remained in this post until his death.

After the fall of the city of New Orleans to Commodore David Farragut, Gutheim was urged to sign the oath of allegiance to the Federal Union, but something about the Southern cause had kindled a flame in his spirit. He refused, was transferred behind Confederate lines, and made his way to Montgomery, Alabama. In 1862, this Jewish immigrant rabbi dedicated the Montgomery synagogue with a prayer expressive of his passionate belief in the lost cause: "Animate all the people of our beloved Confederate States, so as to be equal to all emergencies—ready for every sacrifice, until our cause be vindicated as the light of day."

Confederate Ladies

EUGENIA PHILLIPS and Adah Menken were Jewish ladies who displayed a true devotion to the Southern cause, as well as to their own fiery individualism, even when confronted by the enemy in his own camp. Eugenia was born in Charleston and married Philip Phillips, one of the prominent Southern attorneys of the period. They had moved to Alabama, but when Phillips was elected to Congress, they settled in Washington. They were residing in the federal capital when Fort Sumter was attacked.

Although Phillips was well thought of, a man with influence, his wife fell under suspicion. She and her two daughters, along with her sister Martha Levy, were arrested and held for questioning in the home of a Union lady, Rose

Greenhow. For three weeks the suspect group occupied the attic of the Greenhow house and suffered rough treatment from their captors.

Then Phillips appealed to leading politicos of the day and secured their release. He also got assurance of safe-conduct to Fortress Monroe. The little group set out under Federal guard, crossed the Potomac, and finally made their way to Richmond and the home of Jefferson Davis. There Eugenia delivered documents and maps that she had smuggled out of the Greenhow house in her clothes and in a ball of yarn. Seems that Rose Greenhow, far from being a loyal Union sympathizer, was actually an ingenious spy for the Confederates and was in on the Eugenia deal.

Later in New Orleans, Eugenia ran afoul of the Union commandant of the captured city, General Benjamin "Beast" Butler. She was accused of laughing in public at the sight of a Yankee funeral procession. Eugenia was never one to lean on tact or worry about her own vulnerability. She told General Butler to go to hell and laughed in his face. When informed that she would be sentenced to Ship Island for her conduct, she replied that she took it as a favor, since Butler would not be there.

Several months of captivity on Ship Island, the Devil's Island of its time, reduced Eugenia to a shadow of her former self. When she was finally released, she collapsed in her home, the victim of exhaustion and nervous breakdown. When she recovered, Butler's men asked her to sign the loyalty oath. She refused and, with her husband, left New Orleans and made her way to La Grange, Georgia.

Adah Isaacs was born in Louisiana and at the age of twenty married Alexander Menken of Cincinnati. With the help of her husband, Adah became an actress in one of the stock companies which traveled about from theater to theater. She also wrote poems and essays for the Jewish press. Talented and independent, Adah divorced her husband in an early gesture of Women's Lib and tried her luck on the Broadway stage. Soon she had scored a sensation in *Mazeppa*, in which she played the part of the melodramatic male hero. In 1862 she was playing the part in Baltimore, to packed houses.

The manager was delighted with the proceeds, but not with his temperamental star. Adah insisted that her dressing room be redecorated, which was done. Then she wanted the walls painted Confederate gray, with the Stars and Bars in one corner and pictures of Davis and the Dixie generals all around. The manager protested.

Finally the Federal authorities arrested her. They told her she could either take the oath of loyalty to the Union or leave for Dixie—with one hundred pounds of luggage and no more. Adah made a speech denouncing all such arrangements forever. To get rid of her, they gave her thirty days' probation. The incident was reported all over Baltimore, and now the audiences swelled and cheered the louder in sympathy. She was the darling of the city. A dazzling performer onstage, she had defied the damyankees to their face.

Toward the end of the probation period, she was saved from her own high spirits when she came down with a cold. *Mazeppa* calls for a scene where the hero is stripped down to his skivvies and fastened to a wild horse which drags him (her) off stage. Adah went ahead with the performance that night and by morning had a high fever. She could not get out of bed to report to the Federal officials, tell them to go to hell, and then wind up in the stockade. Instead, she sent word that she was sick and then left for the Jersey coast to convalesce. The illness proved timely and providential, probably saving Adah Menken from imprisonment or transportation behind the Southern lines.

A. C. Myers, Quartermaster General

ABRAHAM C. MYERS, graduate of West Point, scion of a distinguished Jewish family from Charleston, served with General Zachary Taylor in Texas, then in Mexico, and was cited for gallantry in action. He was made chief quartermaster in the army of Mexico and married the beautiful daughter of General David Emanuel Twiggs.

When the Civil War broke out, Myers was commanding the Quartermaster Department at New Orleans. He resigned his commission in the United States Army and late in 1861 was appointed quartermaster general of the Confederate Army.

The problems of this command were overwhelming. First, there were short supplies; then there were short funds. Then there was poor transportation, which sometimes resulted in spoiled food or supplies for the troops. Then there was departmental competition especially with the Ordnance Department, which wanted every scrap of leather the Southern tanners had to offer. Lee's army as a consequence went barefooted more often than it went shod, and the blame fell on the Quartermaster Department. Myers came in for more than the usual amount of criticism and abuse. He was a conspicuous target. Then there was the chain of command and the good old Southern individualism. Myers procured supplies or transportation by hook or by crook, only to have his orders countermanded somewhere along the line. Worst of all was the indifference the rank and file showed to his commands, especially when remote from Richmond headquarters. But disobedience was the plague of the entire Confederacy. More than one historian has offered the opinion that it cost the South a victory in the Civil War.

But what did Myers in and cost him his command was backbiting among the women. Mrs. Myers, the former Marion Twiggs, was both beautiful and sharp-tongued. For some reason she had joined in the group of hens in Richmond that gossiped and criticized Mrs. Jefferson Davis. Marion Myers amused the hen party by calling Mrs. Davis a squaw, which in fact she did resemble and which did indeed make the rounds.

In August, 1863, Jeff Davis issued an order removing Colonel Myers from the Quartermaster Command and replacing him with General A. R. Lawton. The Senators of the Confederacy resisted this move, and it took Davis six months to push it through. Then, as if to humiliate the former commander, Davis ordered Myers to serve under Lawton in the corps. This, of course, Myers refused to do. He was soon relieved of his rank and all standing in the Confederate Army.

Myers lived out the remainder of the war in great want in Georgia. Thereafter the record is obscure. Apparently he traveled through Europe, came home, and died in Washington in 1889. He had very little or no association with other Jews of his time and has been neglected by the historians.

The De Leon Brothers

DAVID CAMDEN DE LEON, like his father before him, studied medicine and became a physician. After graduation he enlisted in the Army and was sent to Florida as a surgeon in the Seminole War. Later, in Mexico with General Zachary Taylor, De Leon displayed heroism far beyond the line of duty. Santa Anna's troops had breached the American defenses at Chapultepec. De Leon jumped in and took command, routing the enemy and saving the position. From then on he was known as the Fighting Doctor and was commended by the United States Congress.

As Civil War approached, David De Leon agonized, like thousands of others in his position, over the question of loyalties. "Treason and patriotism are next door neighbors and only accident makes you strike the right knocker," he wrote to his brother. "I have loved my country, I have fought under its flag, and every star and stripe is dear to me. . . . But I am still convinced that no man can be a patriot who is afraid of being thought a traitor."

De Leon decided in favor of the Confederacy. The family ties with South Carolina went too deep for any other decision. The officer under whom De Leon was serving ordered him to stay with the Federal forces, promised to send him to some remote post away from the fighting, and finally threatened to have him brigged. De Leon slipped out and headed for the border.

Jefferson Davis appointed Dr. De Leon surgeon general of the Confederate Medical Department. This post he held until he was succeeded by Dr. Samuel Preston Moore, who was also of South Carolina. In defeat, Dr. De Leon feared the worst from the conquerors and fled to Mexico. Later Ulysses S. Grant extended an invitation to the medical man in exile to return, which he did. Settled in Albuquerque, New Mexico, where he owned property, Dr. De Leon practiced medicine until his death in 1872. He was fifty-eight years old.

Edwin De Leon, older brother of David, started out practicing law but switched to journalism. Financed by proslavery backers, he edited a newspaper in Washington which expressed the Southern point of view. His support of Franklin Pierce in the 1850's earned him a diplomatic post overseas; he became consul general in Egypt. Here he faced a touchy and dangerous situation. The Turks were harassing the Christians in the Crimea, and a good many innocent victims endured persecution with no one to turn to for redress or protection. Acting on his own initiative, De Leon declared all Greek Christians living in Cairo under the protection of the United States government. Everyone, including the State Department back home, held his breath while awaiting the reaction to this unorthodox and bold measure. The outcome was a sigh of relief. The Turks were intimidated, and the Khedive offered no objection.

On another occasion Consul De Leon displayed similar daring. When several American missionaries were murdered in Palestine, De Leon demanded that the Turkish government capture and deliver the guilty parties. The Turks rounded up five drifters, who were obviously innocent. De Leon threatened to blow the lid off if his request was not given more respect. Finally, the governor produced the assassins, who were tried and put to death.

Because of these and many other successful maneuvers, Washington reappointed De Leon for another term. But when South Carolina seceded, De Leon resigned and offered his services to Jefferson Davis, whom he had known in his old journalism days. Davis appointed De Leon public relations agent and special envoy to European nations. His particular mission was to gain recognition for the Confederacy from France and Great Britain. De Leon got in trouble by opening some secret documents addressed to John Slidell. Then he found favor with the French press. But he got in hot water again by writing proslavery editorials in France. He finally was admitted to the councils of France and England, but he accomplished little or nothing for the Confederacy.

Speaking generally, De Leon was overconfident and was working under the misapprehension that Paris and London were Egypt.

His worst blunder, which cost him his position, not to mention his life savings, came when Federal agents intercepted letters De Leon had written to President Davis. In them he spelled out all his worst fears and blamed everything on Judah P. Benjamin and his corps of diplomats in Europe. These dispatches were published in New York newspapers, with consequences for De Leon that may easily be imagined. He spent the rest of his life earning a meager living as a journalist.

Major Edwin Warren Moise

IN 1832 Edwin Moise was born in Charleston, where several months later a convention would decide that any state might nullify a federal law. His formal schooling ended at fourteen, and the boy went to work, first in a wholesale grocery store, then for two years at the Registry Office, where he could read law at odd hours. Charleston was then plagued with epidemics, and although Edwin enrolled as a volunteer nurse, he escaped smallpox and the more dreaded yellow fever. He started a small business and was doing well enough to marry Esther Lyon, visiting from Petersburg, Virginia, when the great storm of 1855 flooded the store and ruined his prospects.

Charleston had declined in prosperity, and Edwin found it difficult to earn a living for his wife and child. An offer came from Raphael J. Moses of Columbus, Georgia, a prominent lawyer, politician, and plantation owner who had married Edwin's aunt. The Charleston fire of 1837 had put him in the identical situation that confronted Moise. The job called for running the flour mill, keeping books, and what was more important, it enabled him to finish his studies in the Moses law office. The energies of Moise seemed prodigious. The alarm clock would awaken him at four in the morning, and he would read law until six. The tasks on the farm began at seven and lasted all day. Within a short time Edwin became a lawyer and began to practice in his uncle's office.

Success came quickly, and at the outbreak of the war, five years later, Moise was able to spend $10,000, all he had, in organizing a company of 120 cavalrymen which was incorporated into the Confederate Army. Not that he was a fire-eating jingo. Unlike Raphael J. Moses and most of Georgia's public men, he opposed secession in many public speeches, a courageous stand in 1861, but like Robert E. Lee and many others, he went along with his state once war was declared. Public approval of Moise's

efforts in forming this military company was expressed by
the Columbus *Enquirer-Sun* on May 28, 1862, in the
following editorial:

> It will be seen that E. W. Moise has authority to raise a
> company of "Partisan Rangers" and solicits recruits immedi-
> ately. We believe him to be a gentleman well fitted for
> command in this service—cool, but firm and resolute. It is a
> branch of the service that must become highly efficient, and far
> preferable to the gallant soldier to the dull and monotonous
> camp life. We recommend to any who are not enlisted and who
> can enlist to "Book" themselves without delay in Captain
> Moise's list. They will have exciting and useful and perhaps
> profitable work.

After the declaration of peace, Major Moise returned to
Columbus, Georgia, and found the place too desolate to
build on. Having a few relatives in Sumter, he arrived on a
wounded horse and sold it to pay for his family's first
month's board. The war left deep scars in the South. Gone
were the large plantations, the life of leisure and repose.
The ex-soldier remained in Sumter and started anew at the
bottom. Law practice had to be supplemented with farm-
ing. Building houses to replace the ruin and desolation
proved more of a public service than a private gain. Yet all
in all, Major Edwin W. Moise prospered to the extent that
he was able to maintain a summer home at the seashore on
Sullivans Island.

Baron Erlanger Proposes a Plan

JOHN SLIDELL MET the Baron Emile Erlanger, a
Jewish financier, when he was acting as diplomatic agent

for the Confederacy in Paris. They became friends. The baron's son took a fancy to Slidell's daughter, and they became engaged. This romantic mingling of destinies helps explain the baron's desire to assist the Confederate cause.

Knowing that the South needed money desperately, the baron offered to advance a loan of $25,000,000 in hard money. The inside talk hinted that highly placed people in the French government were in on the deal. A bond would be issued, the payment to be made either in cash or in cotton at 12 cents a pound, the going rate at the time in the Confederate States. European investors might rub their hands in expectation over these terms, for the going rate for cotton on the European market was 50 cents a pound. Slidell recognized that this involvement with Southern fortunes and Southern products represented a plus politically for a struggling nation as yet unrecognized in France and England. But he did not trust his own financial know-how and advised Baron Erlanger to travel to Richmond and talk to the Confederates in person.

Davis left the matter in the hands of Secretary of State Benjamin, who reduced the issue from $25,000,000 to $15,000,000 and cut the interest from 8 to 7 percent. The payments in cotton he left alone.

Immediately following the Confederate victory at Fredericksburg, the campaign to sell the bonds commenced. The venture was an instantaneous success. The $15,000,000 issue was oversubscribed the first day. A week later the demand went as high as $80,000,000. Slidell's messages to Benjamin were triumphant. Not only was the current enterprise highly profitable, but European faith in the future of the Confederacy was established.

"An Israelite Without Guile"

ALTHOUGH the North Carolina legislature excluded Jews from holding office in the antebellum period, a high level of tolerance and acceptance was practiced in most areas of the South. Even in North Carolina, as we shall see, the exclusion clause could be and was gotten around when the occasion demanded. In memoirs, letters, histories, and other documents from the period stretching from before the Revolution to after the Civil War, it is clear that the Jews occupied high positions in the Southern states, were popular socially, and intermarried with prominent Gentiles.

The Jews' residency, it should be emphasized, was of long standing. They had come to Georgia and South Carolina almost with the first settlers, so that they had worked the shops and tilled the soil of the South for more than a century before secession. In 1820 at the dedication of a synagogue in Savannah, a visiting dignitary asked: "Have we not cause to exult? On what spot in this habitable globe does an Israelite enjoy more blessings, more privileges, or is more elevated in the sphere of preferment, and more conspicuously dignified in respectable stations?"

Among the earliest elected Senators of the new Republic were David Levy Yulee from Florida and Judah P. Benjamin from Louisiana. We have also observed the number of Jews who occupied high office in the Confederate structure during the war, from Benjamin to A. C. Myers, to De Leon, the surgeon general, and on down the line to many others.

The atmosphere of harmony was particularly in evidence

among the highly cultivated plantation aristocracy, and though no argument or explanation can ever mitigate the slavery which they practiced, it is true that in many respects they were the most civilized class of non-Jews since the days of King Arthur, more so in fact than the last-named, who pursued one another, as well as the "infidel," with sword and spear.

One test of acceptance is the level or degree of intermarriage, which in the antebellum South was fairly high. General David Twiggs of Georgia married his handsome daughter to A. C. Myers. Governor Wickliffe of Kentucky embraced David Levy Yulee as a son-in-law. Kate Davis, related to President Davis, married Joseph Pulitzer, while Judah P. Benjamin took to wife a beautiful Creole girl, Natalie St. Martin of New Orleans. Two daughters of A. C. Myers married into good Gentile families of Virginia. Rachel Lyons of Columbia, South Carolina, married Dr. James F. Heustis in a Richmond ceremony attended by the cream of Southern society. Intimate friendships were formed and perpetuated for life among Jewish and Christian patricians of the South.

From the many informal records of the period, there seems to have been none of the embarrassment or apology that colors any sort of discussion about Jewish matters in the South today. One of my favorite anecdotes from the Civil War period is found in the correspondence of Phoebe Yates Levy Pember, sister of the notorious Confederate supporter Eugenia Phillips. In a letter addressed to Eugenia, Phoebe described the bitter feeling in her circle of friends against the Yankees. During a social evening, Phoebe recounted the number of ladies who thirsted after Yankee blood. One remarked that she had Yankee skeletons brought into her backyard, so that the heap of bones would be the first thing she saw every morning. Another pleaded for a Yankee skull to keep her trinkets in. "At last," Phoebe wrote, "I lifted my voice and congratulated myself at being born of a nation and religion that did not enjoin forgiveness on its enemies, that enjoyed the blessed privilege of praying for an eye for an eye, and a life for a life, and was not one of those for whom Christ died in vain. . . . I proposed that till the war was over they should all join the Jewish church, let forgiveness and peace and good will alone, and put their trust in the sword of the Lord. . . ." Not only were the people present not offended, but most of those in attendance conceded that she had a good argument, "and the gentlemen seconded me ably."

No doubt the Southern gentry were influenced in their attitudes by English Victorian society, which had welcomed the Rothschilds to its high circles and which had elevated Disraeli to political prominence. One suspects that like their English cousins, the Southern aristocrats practiced a snobbery that applied to Jews and Gentiles alike—which is to say, only the best specimens of each were accorded social intimacy or positions of authority. When Jeff Davis was Secretary of War before the Civil War, he appointed three Army officers to study the Crimean War. One of the three appointees was Major Alfred Mordecai. Of this famous soldier Mrs. Jefferson Davis was to write: "He was a Hebrew, and one could readily understand, after seeing him, how that race had furnished the highest type of manhood. . . . His moral nature was as well disciplined as his mental, and his private life was of the purest and most admirable; he was an Israelite without guile."

Even after the war, for as long as the antebellum generation occupied positions of influence, Jews were appointed and elected to high office. But the class that rose with the conclusion of the war and the defeat of the Confederate dream was of a different character. Although the plantation aristocracy survived into the twentieth century, it had lost its power and had gone into decline. (It would appear in the pages of novels by William Faulkner as dignified but decadent.) The new order was more opportunistic, without background, as people used to say, some from the white peasantry with highly emotional race prejudices and an antipathy to people with "foreign blood." In the seats of power a good many demagogues and rabble-rousers now sat, where once the Randolphs, the Calhouns, the Yanceys, and the Davises had been ensconced. Zebulon Vance, the North Carolina governor and U.S. Senator, went around the South delivering a revealing lecture entitled "The Scattered Nation." In it Vance defended the Jews from various common accusations on the grounds that they had suffered persecution and repression for hundreds of years. He spoke about the history of the Jews and the objections raised to their presence in many communities throughout the world. Some of these, said the governor, were serious, and some were trivial; some were deserved, while others were not. And so on. Rather condescending, but still basically sympathetic, Vance's speech was a sure barometer of the change in climate. Where in the antebellum decades the Jews needed no defender or apologetics, in the 1880's they were lucky indeed to have any sort of spokesman from the WASP Establishment.

The shifting prejudices of the Ku Klux Klan were also highly revealing of the changing outlook. During Reconstruction the organization was pledged to the cause of white supremacy in the South. A lingering tradition of religious tolerance made it possible for Jews and Catholics to be members of the night-riding group. General Nathan Bedford Forrest, famous Confederate cavalry leader, was prominent in the activities of the early Klan, which directed its energies against carpetbaggers and scalawags, as well as ambitious blacks. But the later organization, founded by ex-clergyman William J. Simmons, expanded its program to include anti-Catholic and anti-Semitic activity. From 1915 on, in other words, Jews were among the targets of the Klan's operations, and the Klan membership no doubt helped disseminate the anti-Jewish sentiment which still exists in the South. An example of this sort of feeling was evidenced in the bombing of synagogues in Mississippi after the Supreme Court decision of 1954 calling for the desegregation of public schools.

Dostoyevsky once wrote: "The degree of civilization in a society may be judged by entering its prisons." We might add that the degree of civilization of a given society may be judged by the treatment it accords its vulnerable members. If this has any validity, certain nations and time spans in the twentieth century score the lowest grades in recorded history.

Judah P. Benjamin

JUDAH P. BENJAMIN, the "brains of the Confederacy," right-hand man to Jefferson Davis, noted lawyer and sugar planter, delegate to two state constitutional conventions, United States Senator, orator, author, legal authority. One could continue indefinitely. Benjamin was a talented and versatile man with extraordinary intellectual resources. He also had spiritual stamina. He needed it.

Benjamin was born on St. Thomas in the Virgin Islands in 1811. The family came to Charleston, South Carolina, a few years later, and Judah eventually settled in New Orleans, where he applied himself to the practice of law. He proved so proficient by the time he was thirty he was reputed to be the best-known lawyer in the United States.

In the early 1850's he went to the United States Senate, where he pleaded for compromise on the issue of slavery, hoping thereby to avoid secession. "If the Union is divided," he said, "then goodbye to all hopes of the successful attempt of mankind at self-government. The last, the great, the decisive experiment will have failed." From the floor of the Senate, on March 11, 1858, Benjamin delivered the classic defense of slavery. He insisted that slaves were property and that abolitionists were doing neither more nor less than trying to rob Southerners of this property. By including in the Constitution provisions regulating the slave trade and the return of fugitive slaves, the Founding Fathers had clearly indicated slavery was legal. The South based its case on this argument. The argument led Senator Benjamin Franklin Wade of Massachusetts to charge that Benjamin was "an Israelite with Egyptian principles." When Louisiana seceded, Benjamin left the Senate at once and soon accepted the offer of his good friend Jefferson Davis, president of the Confederate States, to serve in the Provisional Cabinet.

During his Senatorial campaign in the 1850's his opponent pointed out that "his forefathers crucified the Saviour." To this irrelevancy Benjamin replied, "When my ancestors were receiving the Ten Commandments from the immediate hand of Deity, the ancestors of my opponent were herding swine in the forests of Great Britain."

Later, out of favor with the rank-and-file Southern

citizens because of military reverses which he could not possibly have controlled, Benjamin suffered the same old illogical stigma. The newspapers said they hoped "to widen the gulf between President Davis and the descendant of those who crucified the Saviour." After the loss of Roanoke Island, Benjamin showed himself more "Christian" than his detractors by offering himself as a scapegoat for the military disaster. He was removed as secretary of war and appointed secretary of state.

Finally he was to become premier of the Confederacy and to engineer the diplomatic policy which hoped to gain recognition in Europe for the Confederate States. His heart was in the Losing Cause as much as any man's, but when the end came, Judah Benjamin fled to England.

With Lee's surrender, Benjamin had escaped from Richmond to Florida in a converted ambulance drawn by a team of worn-out horses. A few months later he was in England, fifty-four years old, penniless, and in poor health. Within six months he was admitted to the British bar, again amassed a fortune, and lived on to become the first American to be made a Queen's Counselor.

He died in Paris in 1884.

Study the life and works of Judah P. Benjamin and you come to one conclusion—he was far to the right of Mark Hanna, Marie Antoinette, and William Buckley. But some of the United Daughters of the Confederacy thought him a Red. *"Gornisht helffen."* (Nothing helps.)

The state of the economy is a big factor in anti-Semitism. In Russia it was the almost unbelievable poverty of the peasant; in France in the 1890's it was the disaster following military defeat and the depression following the Panama Canal swindles; in Germany it was the defeat of the war machine in 1918, the inflation and the economic collapse. And in the state of Georgia in 1913 it was the poverty of the tenant farmer and the frustration of the mill hand who was getting 20 cents an hour in the cotton mills.

My fellow Southerners honor every word, every thought, every battered flag, every gravestone connected with the Confederacy. They have conferred sainthood upon every Confederate from Marse Robert E. Lee himself down to the lowliest drummer boy. They love and cherish them all—all, except one, Judah P. Benjamin. Not a hurrah, not a word. And the interesting paradox about this is that Benjamin, being a Jew, naturally out-Confederated the Confederates. Only he it was who said the South was fighting against the arbitrary confiscation of private property, the black slaves.

A few years ago the Jewish community of Charlotte financed the erection of a stone marker outside the home Benjamin had occupied in the closing days of the Civil War. Soon a letter was circulated among members of the United Daughters of the Confederacy charging Judah P. Benjamin with being a Red, retroactively. The Jews scared and wanted to drop the project, but one staunch pro-Benjamin Daughter of the Confederacy prevailed. When the Jews told her, "We have to live with these people who think Judah P. Benjamin was a Red," this lady said, "Well, have you given thought to the idea that you'll have to live with me, too?"

One woman, and because of her, the marker stands on the main street.

Private Leon of the Charlotte Grays

IN THE RESEARCH ARCHIVES of the Charlotte Public Library I came across the diary of Private Lewis Leon of Charlotte, who enlisted in the Confederate Army when North Carolina seceded from the Union. Private Leon, a sharpshooter in Company B, 53d North Carolina Regiment, fought through three major campaigns until he was finally taken prisoner at the Battle of Spotsylvania Courthouse.

The diary, which was privately published in Charlotte in 1911 by the Stone Publishing Company, contains the rosters of the two companies in which Private Leon served, "Charlotte Grays," Company C, First North Carolina Bethel Regiment, and Company B, 53d Regiment, N.C.T., C.S.A. from Mecklenburg.

After General Lee's surrender, the prisoners of war at the Northern camp at Goshen, New York, were paroled, and Private Leon returned to Charlotte, where he worked as a clerk in a store. Eventually he established his own business. He died in 1919 at Cape Fear Camp, U.D.C., Wilmington, North Carolina, and was buried in the Hebrew Cemetery on McCall Street, in Charlotte, North Carolina.

In 1901, Private Leon sent his diary to the colonel of his regiment, James T. Morehead of Greensboro, who wrote a foreword for the little book and placed his imprimatur on the events, circumstances, and details recorded by Private Leon.

The first entry in the diary is on the date of Leon's enlistment, April 25, 1861:

134

I belong to the Charlotte Grays, Company C, First North Carolina Regiment. We left home for Raleigh. Our company is commanded by Capt. Egbert Ross. We are all boys between the ages of eighteen and twenty-one. We offered our services to Governor Ellis, but were afraid he would not take us, as we are so young; but before we were called out our company was ordered to go to the United States Mint in our town and take same. We marched down to it, and it was surrendered to us. We guarded it several days, when we were ordered to Raleigh, and left on the above date.

We enlisted for six months. Our State went out of the Union on May 20th and we were sent to Richmond, Va., on the 21st. Stayed there several days, when we were ordered to Yorktown, Va. Here they gave us tents to sleep in. This looked more like soldiering, but we would have liked to have had some of that straw in Raleigh. . . .

The first encounter with the Yankees came on June 10, 1861, at Bethel Church, and Leon records it as "the first land battle of the war."

June 10:—At three o'clock this morning the long roll woke us up. We fell in line, marched about five miles, then countermarched, as the Yankees were advancing on us. We got to our breastworks a short time before the Yankees came, and firing commenced. We gave them a good reception with shot and shell. The fight lasted about four hours. Our company was behind the works that held the line where the major of the Yankee regiment, Winthrop, was killed. After he fell our company was ordered to the church, but was soon sent back to its former position. This is the first land battle of the war, and we certainly gave them a good beating, but we lost one of our regiment, Henry Wyatt, who was killed while gallantly doing a volunteer duty. Seven of our men were wounded. The Yankees must have lost at least two hundred men in killed and wounded. It was their boast that they could whip us with cornstalks, but to their sorrow they found that we could do some fighting, too. After the fight some of the boys and myself went over the battlefield, and we saw several of the Yankee dead—the first I had ever seen, and it made me shudder. I am now in a school where sights like this should not worry me long.

Our commander in this fight was Col. Bankhead Magruder. The Yankee commander was Gen. B. F. Butler.

From now on I will never again grumble about digging breastworks. If it had not been for them many of us would not be here now. We returned the same night to Yorktown, full of glory.

Private Leon was discharged at Yorktown and given his passage back to Charlotte. His six months' enlistment period had expired. He loafed for several months, and "On April 23, 1862, I took up arms again for the Old North State and joined a company raised by Captain Harvey White of Charlotte, and left home for the encampment at Weldon.

"June 20:—Col. William Owens is the new commander of the 53rd and we were sworn in, and are now Confederate soldiers for three years or the whole war period." The regiment then began its long campaign northward, across the Tar River, the Rapidan, through Virginia, across the Potomac, into Maryland and eventually to Pennsylvania. All through the diary, Private Leon shows a rare talent for carefully reporting all details concerning marches, "foraging expeditions," and battles. He also had a sense of humor.

"July 4:—This is the day the Yankee General McClellan promised to eat dinner in our capitol. He did not, but many of his command did, in our prisons, and they did not eat turkey."

In emphasizing his ability to sleep under any and all conditions, Private Leon usually wrote: ". . . and so I flopped down and slept better than Abe Lincoln."

Leon's closest buddies were Jacob Katz and Hugh Sample, both of Mecklenburg County. "When it comes to foraging for food," Leon records, "Liet. Belk trusts the three best foragers in the business—Katz, myself, and Hugh Sample. He mentions that "Sample is one of the four Samples in our Regiment. There are also four Alexanders, not counting officers, four Wilsons, and three Trotters."

Leon writes of General Robert E. Lee with deep emotion and affection. On several occasions in the diary he refers to the Confederate commander as "our father."

"Sept. 19:—This morning they read an order from our father R. E. Lee in which he gave furlough into Richmond of all Israelites in honor of the Jewish New Year. Wortheim, Oppenheim, Norment, Katz and myself, as well as Liet. E. Cohen, worshipped."

The Charlotte Grays were in the forefront of the march into Pennsylvania, where all the roads seemed to lead to Gettysburg.

Private Lewis Leon, an immigrant boy, closed his diary with an entry on April 25, 1865, in the form of a declaration of his devotion to duty in his adopted and beloved land:

> The four years that I have given to my country I do not regret, nor am I sorry for one day I have given. My only regret is that we have lost for what we have fought. Nor do I think for one moment that we lost it by any other means than by being outnumbered at least five if not ten to one. The world was open to them, and closed to us. I was not quite nineteen when I went in, and now I am twenty-three years old, and I shall say again that although but a private I did my duty, and I believe our Cause was just.

Private Leon came alone to America from Germany. He

was sixteen years old at the time of his arrival here, and the reason he came to Charlotte was that he had an uncle who had a store in Charlotte and that's where he got a job. He left his father and mother back in Germany, and he never saw them again, although he corresponded with them frequently. His father was a butcher and a good Orthodox Jew. Thus Private Leon, an immigrant boy, closed his diary with an entry on April 25, 1865.

Poison Enters the System

As WE HAVE SEEN, for the most part relations between Christians and Jews in the antebellum South were harmonious. Jews were not only an integral but a significant part of the life of the region. They participated in the social, economic, political, and artistic life of their communities and, in fact, in many cases were leaders of such activities.

With the advent of the Civil War, it is likewise evident that Jews played an active role in the military and financial support of the Confederacy. There were of course the inevitable accusations and challenges to the positions occupied by prominent Jews, but these were isolated cases, usually unsupported by public opinion.

As the Civil War dragged on, with its growing list of dead and injured, with the shortage of food and supplies, as well as dwindling hopes, demoralization became mixed with a sort of desperate anger. These are the exact conditions that have led men in many different regions of the globe to seek out a scapegoat. Almost always, when the atmosphere has been properly established, an opportunist steps forth and says what the people are waiting to hear.

There were few enough "foreigners" in the Civil War South to fill the bill. The Yankees were too remote, and besides, everyone was tired of cursing the Yankees. It had become a stale sport. The blacks were an obvious target, but even with the renunciation of logic it seemed far-fetched to place the blame on the slaves of the plantation owners, especially since many blacks had remained faithful to their jobs during the war and had continued to work the plantation in the master's absence.

In the 1840's and '50's Henry S. Foote had been Senator and governor of Mississippi, and during the war he was serving as member of the Confederate Congress. Foote had a rigid personality with tendencies toward violence. He had fought several duels, and once he had actually traded blows with Jefferson Davis, with whom he disagreed on certain issues. Today perhaps we would find a suitable term for Foote in our stock of terms borrowed from the vocabulary of psychiatry. But in the general madness of the 1860's a few more mad pronouncements not only were considered normal, but were readily accepted.

And so Henry Foote commenced his campaign of anti-Semitic slander. The United States, he claimed, is dominated and controlled by Jews. They own most of the property in the South, and by the outcome of the war the Jews below the Mason-Dixon Line will wind up owning everything. At present, all these Jewish conspirators are under the protection of Judah P. Benjamin. Foote's deepest fear, which he referred to on many occasions, was that if the South should win, Benjamin would become chief justice of a Southern Supreme Court.

An early avatar of the late Joe McCarthy, Foote was always threatening to expose Benjamin and other members of the Jewish conspiracy but never produced a shred of evidence against anyone. When a Richmond newspaper reported that a member of the Confederate Congress had accepted a bribe to procure passports for three Jews who wanted to cross over to the Union lines, Foote demanded that a committee be formed to investigate the outrage. The committee was appointed and found nothing to substantiate the story. Even the reporter who had written the dispatch had no details. The editor had in fact forbidden publication, but somehow the piece had slipped in.

Henry Foote's patriotism for the Confederacy took a curious turn. As the war drew to a close, he went over to the enemy, after the war supported the national Republican administrations, and was appointed superintendent of the United States Mint in New Orleans in 1878. He died in 1880.

But he had set the contagion going, and other Southern politicians caught the virus. Congressmen from Alabama, South Carolina, and Florida perpetuated the myths of conspiracies and treachery and immediate danger to all Gentiles. Officers in the Confederate Army tried to block the promotion of Jewish subalterns. The anti-Semite, if sincere in his beliefs, must live in a state of continual fear that this basically peace-loving minority will rise up and take away everything he owns. His own delusions are in effect his punishment.

Judah Benjamin bore the brunt of much of it. He himself had married a Catholic and had no connections with temple or synagogue—in fact had few Jewish friends. But because of his eminence in the Confederate structure, he became a likely target for the hate mongers—those who not only hated Benjamin and the Jews, but resented Jeff Davis and the Cause and the awful situation in which they found themselves. So Benjamin was the "Hebrew of the Hebrews" or "the Jew Benjamin" who was leading the South to its destruction. Davis kept a cool head throughout the whole thing. He knew that the attacks on Benjamin were simply a manifestation of concealed bitterness about the Confederacy and its President.

John B. Jones, a clerk of the Confederate War Department stationed in Richmond, left a diary full of anti-Semitic slurs. The man was obsessed. "They have injured the cause more than the armies of Lincoln." Benjamin and Myers were traitors. Jones wrote poison-pen letters in his diary throughout the war.

In the South newspapers began to print accusations about the Jews' role in scarcity of goods and inflation. The charges grew to the proportion of libel and vilification. As Mark Antony says: "Mischief, thou art afoot. Take thou what course thou wilt."

Dr. Simon Baruch and Son Bernard

OF THE MANY HUNDREDS of Jewish soldiers who served the Confederacy in the Civil War, two names are deserving of special mention. One is that of Max Frankenthal, who fought in the Mississippi Infantry. Frankenthal (whose name was sometimes given as Fronthall or Frauenthal) started out his military career as a drummer, but soon joined in the action. In May, 1864, the Union forces under Grant besieged Lee at the famous Battle of Spotsylvania Courthouse. The hottest spot would later be called the

Bloody Acute Angle, and it was here that Frankenthal, the drummer boy, was observed loading and firing at the enemy for twenty straight hours, under the most terrible musket fire of the entire war. An observer later wrote that little Max stood in the midst of it, cool, unflinching, and constant. Years later Confederate soldiers picked up the expression "a regular Fronthall"—meaning a man distinguished by his courage. The pronunciation was a bit off, but the spirit of the thing was right. They meant it as a tribute to Max Frankenthal, the drummer boy of the Mississippi Infantry.

One of the most interesting men of the period, in and out of war, was Dr. Simon Baruch, who came to the United States as a lad of fifteen and worked in the shop of a relative living in Camden, South Carolina. Simon went to med school at Charleston and later at Richmond. Upon graduation he enlisted in the Confederate Army and was given the rank of assistant surgeon. He served with the Third South Carolina Battalion, was twice taken prisoner and twice exchanged and returned to active duty. During one period he worked on the wounded without rest until he collapsed from exhaustion. When he was captured and held prisoner at Fort McHenry, he sat down and wrote a monograph on chest wounds which is still valued.

"South Carolina," he told his colleague Dr. Benjamin Taylor, "gave me all I have. I'll go with my state." So he was off for Second Manassas with the men of Kershaw's Brigade, stopping only to caution his seventeen-year-old brother, just over from Prussia, to keep out of the fighting. When they met again, nine months later, the youngster was wearing the uniform of a Confederate cavalryman.

He was discharged at the end of the conflict, married,

and settled down in Camden, South Carolina, for fifteen years. In 1881 he moved to New York.

In 1915 Simon Baruch sat down and wrote his memoirs under the title *Reminiscences of a Confederate Soldier*. In 1917 he informed his friends that he regretted that he was too old to serve his country again, this time in World War I. He stood ready, he said, to devote himself, his entire spirit and resources to the defense of the country he had adopted, which for sixty years had "enhanced and protected my life, honor, and happiness." Dr. Baruch died in 1921, a dedicated military man, physician, and public servant. His son, Bernard Baruch, became adviser to Presidents and a household name signifying the dignity of political office.

Dr. Baruch had married Belle Wolfe of Camden, and they had five children, sons Hartwig, Bernard, Herman, Sailing, and daughter Renee. The first three boys were born in Camden, the other two children were born in Charleston, South Carolina. In New York son Bernard adjusted well, but even in boyhood Bernard began to realize "the bottomless chasm that separated the white and black races," and for him it was a shattering revelation. It was not something he learned at home. Never there did he hear the term "nigger"; never from his father and mother did he hear a word derogatory to blacks. He could not understand why it was that Frank and the butler's daughter Henrietta were "different," why his playmates could be his playmates no more. Like thousands of Southern white children before him and since, Bernard was caught in that tangled web of racial relations which lets the white child drink its milk from the black woman's breast but denies her the use of his drinking fountain. It was the dilemma of the whole South.

"Nigger, nigger," was the cry they hurled at the Southern boys, pouncing always upon the weakest of them. The ringleader was an Irish boy named Johnson. Hartwig, the oldest brother, thrashed him and thrashed him again, whipping him at last on the school steps. Whimpering, Johnson tattled to his teacher, and Hartwig was suspended from school.

But what a hero he was in Bernard's eyes! Hartwig was at his side when, hounded and outnumbered, the Baruch boys fled up the steps of their boardinghouse, with shouts and rocks flying after them. Then came a new word— "sheeny." They did not know what it meant. They had never heard it before.

The historical and ethical precepts of his faith, more than the strictly religious doctrines, stirred the father Dr. Baruch. He was a charter member and president of the Hebrew Benevolent Association, the only organized Jewish group in town, and his beautiful letter of resignation in the winter of 1880 illumines the philosophy that would be reflected so vividly by his famous son.

The doctor's major field of interest was in hydrotherapy —the treatment of certain ills with water. On this subject Dr. Baruch wrote two books which were considered the authority of the period. His interest in hydrotherapy logically extended outward to the area of sanitation and health, and in 1901 he was instrumental in establishing the first public bath in America. It was located on Rivington Street on the Lower East Side of New York City and is still in use. Around the same time, Dr. Baruch was appointed to the Saratoga Commission and helped design and restore Saratoga Mineral Springs. He worked voluntarily, without compensation, guiding the commission in its construction of the health resort.

Equally revolutionary were the doctor's ideas on treatment for the common and usually fatal complaint then known familiarly as "inflammation of the bowels." Ever since the Civil War, surgeons had begun to open and cleanse the abdominal cavity, but it was Dr. Baruch who insisted on the revolutionary theory that the cause of the trouble, the appendix, should be removed whether already ruptured or not. This was a revolutionary idea to a pair of fellow surgeons called in to consult with Dr. Baruch over a sinking patient.

"He will die if we do," said one of the doctors flatly, shaking his head. "He will die if we don't," Dr. Baruch answered. He was later credited with being the "first doctor in the world to diagnose, pre-operatively, a case of ruptured appendix, in which successful operation was performed and the patient lived." Speaking before the New York Academy of Medicine in 1894, the noted surgeon Dr. John A. Wyeth, himself a Confederate veteran, declared: "The profession and humanity owe more to Dr. Baruch than to any other one man for the development of surgery of appendicitis."

Miss Belle, too, adapted herself quickly to life in New York. Here were organizations that she could enjoy, even a Wade Hampton Chapter of the United Daughters of the Confederacy. A born "joiner," in her mature years she was regent of the Knickerbocker Chapter of the Daughters of the American Revolution, president of the Washington Headquarters Club and of the Southland Club of New York.

City College in the 1880's was at Twenty-third Street and Lexington Avenue, where today the towers of the Bernard M. Baruch School of Business and Public Administration poke their way into the sky. Here the whole little world of the college revolved, with a campus of busy paved streets, but with an occasional glimpse of old Gramercy Park with its rose-brick houses frilled in iron lace.

Bernard Baruch eventually became a Wall Street speculator, where he was called the Lone Eagle. Men turned to whisper as he passed, runs a highly colored account of Baruch at the end of the century, "tall, aquiline, smiling, but uncommunicative among the excited stock dealers." He was alone. He was always alone. He was deaf to tips, indifferent to advice or information. Ruefully, Otto Kahn, no mean moneymaker himself, told the story of the young Baruch bursting out to him the instant they shook hands not to tell him any market rumors—they might confuse his own judgment.

His self-confidence might have been laughable had it not been so justified. To hardened old-timers Baruch seemed a part of the eternal mystery of Wall Street. They did not know the hours and years of study he had spent on subjects unfamiliar to him, the patient sifting of the trivial for the bedrock of fact, the soul-searching, the self-discipline that had produced the phenomenon that was Bernard Baruch. They called it genius; he knew it to be, in large part, hard work.

Baruch was a success at his profession, so amazing a success that his legend has persisted for fifty years. It is true that he did go broke once or twice before his fortunes stabilized, and this would be due to the violation of his own rules. The rules worked; there was no magic secret to the game. There were other wonder boys in Wall Street, like Morton Schwartz, who came out of Louisville, Kentucky, to make a million before he was twenty. But Baruch was one of the few successful speculators of his generation, not so much because of what he made as because of what he was able to keep. Not his services as Presidential adviser, or his relations with the New Deal, or his behind-the-scenes exploits as "elder statesman," but "how he made his potatoes" is of primary interest to the public mind. He was the American dream come true. He was the American success story, the aspiration fulfilled of every young man off the farms, or out of the little towns and villages, who dreamed of conquering the city and of amassing wealth and fame and power. If he did it, maybe they could too. And so they dreamed, forgetful that the rules change in fifty years and that even the game itself would be recognizable no longer.

Many versions of Baruch's rules of success have been given. It would take a book to list them all. Yet it is possible to reduce them to general principles. It was no question of blind jumps in the dark. To be a successful trader you would have to (1) know mankind, (2) know yourself, (3) know your world and your time, (4) know the stock, the market, and the rules of the game.

It was possible, Baruch admitted, to make money and be wrong—some of the time. If you were right five times out of eight, you could make money. If you were right only six times out of ten, you could make a good deal of money, and if you knew how to retrench and cut your losses, you could make money, even if you were right only two or three times out of ten. Baruch was right far more.

It was not the lure of moneymaking alone that held him enthralled with the Street for so many years. It was the thrill of the game. Wall Street was legalized gambling and would endure so long as the love of something for nothing was inherent in humankind. You could control the excesses of Wall Street; you could not redirect the course of human nature.

Baruch had once forgotten Yom Kippur, the Day of Atonement—that belonged entirely to his home and family. And on Yom Kippur no business could be transacted.

Baruch went home to observe his holiday. On Monday the telephone began to ring, and it rang all day. Baruch never lifted the receiver from the hook. After a while the calls ceased.

What happened? The stock had opened at 100, dropped to 97, then rallied. Had Baruch been there, he would have given orders to sell out. But he was not there. In the afternoon the stock sagged again. Eventually it dropped to 60. And when Baruch did close out the next September, his profits were some $700,000.

The newly elected President Wilson looked to Baruch for advice on financial, farm, and defense problems.

The Council of National Defense was composed exclusively of Cabinet officers, but an Advisory Commission to the council was appointed by the President and became its operative part. The first official meeting of the Advisory Commission was held in a Washington hotel room on the evening of December 7, 1916, in an atmosphere of uncertainty and confusion, no one quite knowing why he was there or what was expected of him. The membership was made up of the lean, classic-featured Dr. Franklin Martin, director general of the American College of Surgeons; Julius Rosenwald of Sears, Roebuck, a "prince of a good fellow" who made you like him more with each passing day; the president of the Baltimore and Ohio Railroad, Daniel Willard, with alert blue eyes and outthrust lower lip; Howard Coffin, vice-president of the Hudson Motor Company, all ideas and ideals; Dr. Hollis Godfrey, president of the Drexel Institute of Philadelphia, who had been one of the earliest proponents of industrial mobilization;

Bernard Baruch; and the man who above all interested the others, the aging, leonine Samuel Gompers.

For none of his associates could Baruch ever feel quite the warmth he had for the "graduates" of the War Industries Board, except for those few who, like himself, served Woodrow Wilson closely—Grayson, Glass, Daniels, Mac-Adoo. One of the great Southern newspapers, the Raleigh *News and Observer*, survived the Depression years because of Baruch, who assured the editor, Josephus Daniels, that his help to Daniels had been to him a great pleasure.

And out of Baruch's service with Wilson came his warmest friendship of all—with Winston Churchill. Baruch was frank in telling the great Englishman how much he meant to him. In later years, during the dark struggle of atomic crisis, Churchill returned the tribute: "I value greatly your long memorable friendship. I am very thankful you have your present great responsibilities, and I sleep more soundly in my bed because I know the sentinel is awake."

All these diverse activities provided no real outlet for Baruch's tumultuous energies, and the most alluring prize of all dangled always and forever beyond him. Not *every* American boy could dream of growing up to become President. A man past eighty, seated on the portico of Hobcaw Barony, looking through the white columns to the impersonal sweep of Winyah Bay beyond, Baruch once murmured wistfully, "I could have been President of the United States—if I had not been a Jew."

Whether or not he was right, he thought he was. The fact is, his being a Jew may have provided a comfortably satisfying excuse for his not becoming President. It was true that he had emerged as a keyman in the Wilson era, that even former President Theodore Roosevelt hailed him as the ablest man in the administration. Baruch believed also that Al Smith could have been President had he not been a Catholic. But in 1928, as in 1936, the people were not prone to shoot Santa Claus. The prosperity of the twenties was Republican prosperity; it is doubtful that any Democrat could have been elected in the wave of "normalcy." As for Baruch he had other strikes against him. "The Sidewalks of New York," for all their limitations, undeniably had more political appeal than Wall Street, and although Baruch may have emerged from the war a keyman to those in the know, he was no hero to the average, hard-shooting, narrow-thinking, small-town doughboy, who cursed the "foreign" ammunition he was given to use and looked, in vain, for American weapons that never came. Justly or unjustly, Baruch bore much of the blame for this deficiency and was still blamed by the veterans a generation and more afterward.

In 1932 the Democratic nominee for the Presidency of the United States waved his arm. "This is the Brain Trust, Bernie, and you're the Professor Emeritus."

His head grazing the doorway of the tiny study at Hyde Park, Bernard Baruch scanned the faces before him. There was Louis Howe, long ears dragging his collars, deepset spaniel eyes gazing mournfully. There, too, was Professor Raymond Moley of Columbia, slant-eyes narrowed in suspicion, and his colleague, the curly-headed and boyish Rexford G. Tugwell. Sitting in was Baruch's and Roosevelt's old friend, Judge Samuel Rosenman. This was the original Brain Trust. Later there would be additions and substitutions. The limits of Baruch's participation were set by the President-elect in his introduction. Baruch was never to be "quite in the inner circle, not in the real Brain Trust." His correspondence reveals that he saw the nominee only

Dr. Simon Baruch and Son Bernard

three times between the convention and the twentieth of December. His role had been cast: adviser to the advisers, elder statesman without portfolio.

Baruch had come to accept the inevitability of war. In the spring of 1941, as an uproar sounded over a White House bill to commandeer property for national defense, Baruch gave Roosevelt complete support. There was a need to "club into line a small group" that was seeking "self gains in selfish ways."

Production would win a war, and once the United States shifted into high gear, Baruch had no fear of Germany. Mechanized warfare was our dish of tea, and he realized how the news that we were at last swinging into action would impress Hitler.

For Baruch, as for Roosevelt, for Stimson, for all who had known the nightmare of the spring of 1940, the attack on Pearl Harbor was like the bursting of a giant abscess. Everyone might still be "running around at loose ends in Washington," but at least now with the unity of a single purpose. Even the isolationists, who were moved primarily by any civilized man's hatred of war, could lend their idealism to the common cause. Republicans took their place in the councils. At the suggestion of Felix Frankfurter, Colonel Henry L. Stimson was brought out of retirement to be Secretary of War—Stimson, who had held his first Cabinet seat under William Howard Taft and had spotted the outbreak of the Second World War back in Manchuria nearly thirteen years before. With him came Colonel Frank Knox, a man who had offered him support, and was wise enough to accommodate himself to a President with a personal interest in the Navy. "Jim" Forrestal of Dillon, Read and Company, a Dutchess County Democrat and Baruch's friend, was also one of the "inside men."

DEAR BERNIE,

For a long time I have been calling upon you for assistance in questions affecting our war production. You have given unsparingly of your time and energy and your advice has been exceedingly valuable. I know that you have preferred to serve in an advisory capacity and have been disinclined to accept an appointment . . . to an administrative position. However, I deem it wise to make a change in the direction of War Production and I am coming back to the elder statesman for assistance. I want to appoint you as Chairman of the War Production Board with power to direct the activities of the organization.

To the nation Bernard Baruch was the "Park Bench Statesman." But to official Washington during those years of the Second World War, he was "the tall old trouble-shooter." There in Lafayette Square he sat, spring and autumn alike, bundled in a heavy overcoat. His bench, to which mail was duly addressed and delivered, was just off dead center of the park, near the rear end of the equestrian statue of Andrew Jackson. It was four feet six inches long, just big enough to accommodate Baruch and one average-sized Cabinet officer. Hard candy sometimes rattled in his pockets, but it was for himself, not for the pigeons or squirrels.

He rarely caused a ripple in the quiet life of the park. It was as if he belonged there, along with the newspaper photographers and the loafers, the government employees on lunch hour, the lovers, the nursemaids and the children. Pigeons rooted around his high-laced shoes. Tourists saun-tered by to smile and to snap pictures of Jackson, rearing ever upward on his bronze-green charger. Once Baruch dropped his gold watch, and it was later returned by a child who was playing nearby, to whom he presented a war bond.

After that the children played even nearer, hoping that he would drop something again.

He was a part of the park, this shrewd old man whose eyes had seen the follies of two world wars, looking, according to press accounts, "like Michelangelo's Moses turned buccaneer" or like an "old wind-blown eagle." These expressions were typical. During the 1940's the public press gushed forth fountains of almost cloying hero worship of Baruch, for which the elder statesman, despite his disclaimers of superpowers or superprescience, cannot be held wholly irresponsible. He had too carefully culti-vated his friendship with the top moguls of journalism for that. Nevertheless, there was another and more valid reason for this hero worship of the elder statesman, which in-creased steadily toward the decade's end. Looking back over the last quarter of a century, we can see that after the national collapse of 1929, the country sought a father image. Franklin Roosevelt filled the bill capably, but there also was Baruch, who, if a little old for the father role, was at least "the granddaddy of them all," and the veneration in which he was held was reflected by the nickname, Old Uncle Sam, the national symbol itself. Then, too, and always, there must be remembered what Sherwood Ander-son has termed "the myth of greatness." He points out that "most modern great men are mere illusions sprung out of a national hunger for greatness." As the politicians of the industrial age have created myths about themselves, so too have the financiers, the millionaires perhaps most of all. And finally, as Anderson says, they themselves are "chil-dren enough to believe the myth" they created. And if they believe it, why should not all America?

Harry S. Truman looked small and uncertain in that

Presidential chair. He sat before the desk in the Oval Office, his back to the sun and the iron gates where the people had massed in silence through the April night. "Here was change," the greatest change, perhaps, since Lincoln had died. As he has said, the sun and the moon and the planets had fallen on him. The prison of the Presidency had closed around him. Scarcely fifteen hours before, history had broken into a gathering in Speaker Sam Rayburn's office, and Truman, dazed after his summons to the White House, had placed a call to his own apartment. Mr. Truman later appointed Baruch to head the Atomic Energy Commission to the United Nations, where Mr. Baruch opened his address to that body with these famous words: "We are here to judge between the quick and the dead."

Many of the basic formulas of the Baruch Plan were in his report: the demand for "inspection" of atomic facilities and not just the outlawing of war or potential atom-war activities; the stipulation that any plant engaged in manufacturing of a dangerous nature must be owned and operated by an International Atomic Development Authority; the stipulation that at some point our manufacture of bombs must cease and the transfer of atomic information to the authority proceed in stages; and most important of all, perhaps, the recognition that there was no real military defense against the atomic bomb, and that to safeguard ourselves there must be no immediate surrender of atomic knowledge.

Actually, Baruch's reputation for wisdom and disinterested patriotism had so grown over the years that his influence depended but little on Presidential approval. Even after a break with Truman he was making arrangements for consultations with Stuart Symington, Secretary of the Air Force; Louis Johnson, Secretary of Defense; Lewis Strauss of the Atomic Energy Commission; and David Lilienthal, among many others in high office. General Omar Bradley, Senator Wayne Morse, Secretary John Snyder, all wrote Baruch of their dependence on him for advice and counsel.

And on the bench in Lafayette Square, he still sat, dispensing nuggets of wisdom in the sunlight. "Now, in the afternoon of my life, I reaffirm my faith in this country of ours—this infinitely potent, this quick-rewarding, this slow-to-anger, bold, independent, just and loving mother of us all. We oppose slavery, whether imposed by the state or the individual."

Although at the last there was no real reconciliation, even before the "pleasant chat" at General Marshall's, at the suggestion of Anna Rosenberg and Marshall, President Truman offered Baruch a place on the Universal Military Training Commission. Again the elder statesman, now approaching eighty-one, pleaded his age and declined. In later years, when asked if he would go to Washington if called by Truman, he replied, as he always would have replied, "Of course. You don't turn down a call from the President."

He knew well enough, however, that no call would come. He could be content with an expression of faith from Mrs. Roosevelt, who in a handwritten note said, "You have done all you could for your country. God bless you, dear, kind friend."

Penina Moise, Poet

MANY OF THE HYMNS which are used today in the
Reform temples of America were written by Penina Moise.
She was born in Charleston in 1807 and died in 1880.
Penina was the daughter of Abraham Moise, founder of the
family, and, although handicapped with poor vision, never-
theless acquired an education. Edward Saveth writes of
Penina:

> She published in 1833 a volume of poems entitled *Fancy's
> Sketch*, and wrote for newspapers and periodicals in Washing-
> ton, Boston, New York, and New Orleans. Among her works
> are numerous hymns, recitations, and poems for Sunday school
> use. Penina was for a time superintendent of the Sunday school
> of Beth Elohim Congregation of Charleston. A volume of
> hymns written for this congregation went through four large
> editions. These supplemented but did not displace a series of
> hymns written for the congregation by Cordelia Moise (b.
> 1809; d. 1869), daughter of Cherie and Hetty Cohen Moise.
>
> The poems of Penina Moise are written for the most part in
> a light vein, and reveal much humor and a clever play on
> words. *Fancy's Sketch Book* is typical of the style. Sometimes
> more serious themes attracted her. Her *Invocation to Frost* was
> written when the yellow fever scourge struck Charleston in
> 1854.
>
> While her brothers and nephews were fighting in the armies
> of the Confederacy she composed a stirring war song entitled
> "Cockades of Blue" that was a true measure of her devotion to
> the secessionist cause. When Charleston was attacked she was
> compelled to take refuge with her sister Rachel and her niece,
> Jacqueline Levy, in the town of Sumter. With the coming of
> peace, they returned to Charleston, where they established a

school. This was maintained until shortly before her death. In her seventy-third year, although troubled by blindness and neuralgia, she asked:

> "But why should I not wish to linger here?
> Do I not dwell in friendship's atmosphere?
> Where generous souls such balmy tribute bring
> As makes my wintry age so like to spring
> That scarce the blind recluse, amid its snows,
> Detects the absence of the vernal rose?"

"A Book on the Schwartzers"

THE JEWISH PEDDLERS who sold on credit to the blacks called it having "a book on the Schwartzers," which meant carrying a ledger sheet for a black customer. "Schwartzers," which means "the blacks," was not a sign of disrespect. As a matter of fact, the Jewish peddler performed a great service for the blacks of the South between the years 1900 and 1920. They were probably the first white people in the South who paid the black people any respect at all, who regarded them as equals. A customer is an equal, and when you sell a person merchandise on credit, you respect him. Some of the white merchants sold to black tenant farmers on credit, but this was an entirely different thing. They sold him seed and a mule and whatever else he may have needed for his crop, but they sold to him on credit only on the same ledger sheet with the name of the farmer from whom the black was renting or for whom he was sharecropping. The "boss man," as the black called the white farmer, had to go surety on the credit for the black's supplies. But with the "book on the Schwartzers," the Jewish peddler put the black's family name in the book, and they let them try on the merchandise, and once the peddler learned the names, he did not say "Uncle" or "Auntie" or "boy" but "Mr." or "Mrs.," whatever their names.

Why did so many Jewish immigrant boys and men take to peddling? Well, for them it was the quickest way to get started in America. Because they could not speak the language and probably looked "different," too, they had no chance at all in the employment market. Therefore, instead of "presenting" themselves to the open society, they "presented" their merchandise. Thus they could learn the language and the ways of America and earn a living at the same time. And they could start earning the day after they got off the boat. Many thousands of young peddlers merely used the trade to "get a start," to earn enough to start a business or to finance an education.

And the one peddler who received the most welcome reception, who met few hostile farmers or trouble of any kind, was the Jewish peddler in the South who began to come in substantial numbers in the 1880's. Because the Jewish peddler began to deal with the blacks and the rural sharecroppers, he eliminated himself as serious competition for the local storekeeper. Not until some forty years later was the local storekeeper interested in the black trade. But the important reason for the peddler's happiness in the South—the Bible Belt—was his religion. The Anglo-Calvinist culture was Fundamentalist in its Protestantism, with heavy emphasis on the books of the Old Testament. In small towns and rural communities where probably no one had ever seen a Jew before, the peddler was the "living witness" of Biblical truth, and many people were particularly anxious to have him as a lodger for the night. The peddler himself may not have been aware of it, but for these Fundamentalist Protestants he bore identity with Moses, Isaiah, Jeremiah, and the Second Coming. He would be asked questions about the Bible, and in this he was fortunate. Most peddlers started out at the age of sixteen, some a year or so earlier. These young boys were still steeped in the Orthodoxy and Judaistic legalisms of their upbringing. The Southern farmers listened to them with respect and looked forward to their coming.

The late Harry Richter of Mount Gilead, North Carolina, lived through this pleasant experience of the Jewish peddler in the South. We had many conversations before he died, and we had exchanged many letters. Richter began peddling in the South at the turn of the century, and he tells of a home that became a boardinghouse for peddlers.

"It was the home of the Haywoods in Montgomery County of North Carolina. They offered me lodging for the night, the first time I met them, which I gladly accepted. It was quite evident that the Haywoods were poor, earning their livelihood from a none too impressive farm. Cotton was selling at twenty-five dollars a bale and corn in proportion, but the Haywoods displayed a curious interest in me, and particularly the lady of the house, Malissa Haywood. Conversation was difficult. I was barely three months in the country, but we got along. I was peddling in that county at that time and I got back to my lodgings for the weekend, for the Sabbath. The letters I got from home [Russia], written in Yiddish, had to be read aloud in the original. The Haywoods wanted to hear the language. They wanted to hear the sound of it. Then it had to be translated word for word. Mrs. Haywood frequently reminded me of my duties toward my parents on the 'other side,' and she was more emphatic when she reminded me of my duties to my religion. The Haywoods loved to listen to me recite the morning and evening prayers.

"Later on, other peddlers stopped there for the night or for the weekend, and eventually the dietary observances of us Jewish peddlers were looked after most carefully. The biscuits were prepared without lard, and the eggs were kept at a safe distance from the inevitable porker, of which there were always several varieties on the table. There were many such families in the Carolinas, Virginia, and Georgia at the turn of the century. And many peddlers, like myself, mere youngsters, fresh from the last embrace of their mothers and left alone with their fears and longings, found great comfort in these religious people of the South. In other parts of the country peddlers have told me that we were nothing more than mere laughable individuals with a foreign accent, but not in the South. In the South, the orthodox Protestants granted us dignity; they were the first to make us feel that we really belonged."

The Cherokee called the peddler (phonetically at least), *jew-wedge-du-gish*, literally, "the egg eater." The Jewish peddler often found it necessary to refuse food offered him in all kindliness because it had not been prepared in accordance with kosher dietary laws. Wherever he went he asked for eggs in barter. He carried hard-boiled eggs in his pockets and existed on a diet of eggs and vegetables when away from home or his base of supplies. Many of the Jewish peddlers arranged their routes to bring them home Thursday night, ensuring that an unscheduled delay did not keep them on the road until too late to make proper preparation for the Sabbath.

Because the German peddler had trouble with the English language owing to his guttural, heavy accent, the

Rabbi James K. Gutheim, a true Confederate rabbi.

Rabbi Maximilian J. Michelbacher, Beth Ahabah Congregation, Richmond, Virginia.

Adah Menken, a spy for
the Confederacy.

Eugenia Phillips, a spy
for the Confederacy.

Edwin Warren Moise, in Confederate uniform.
Born 1832.

Rebecca Gratz, Sir Walter Scott's inspiration for Rebecca in *Ivanhoe*. (*Painting by Thomas Sully.*)

Dr. Simon Baruch. 1840–1921.

Moses Ezekiel. Among the best known of his statues is "Religious Liberty," commissioned by the B'nai B'rith in 1876. 1844–1917.

Isidor Straus, philanthropist and merchant. 1845–1912.

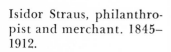

Colonel B. F. Jonas, United States Senator from Louisiana.

Dr. Joseph Goldberger, who found the cure for pellagra. 1874–1929.

Herman Cone, founder of
the Cone Mills Corporation.
1820–1897.

Moses H. Cone, co-founder
of Cone Mills. 1857–1908.

Caesar Cone, co-founder of Cone Mills. 1859–1917.

Benjamin Cone, retired chairman of the board.

Herbert H. Lehman, four times governor of New York and twice Senator of that state. 1878–1963.

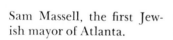

Sam Massell, the first Jewish mayor of Atlanta.

Jewish peddler who followed him was also called a Dutch peddler. For the Americans, the accent sounded similar, which indeed it was. An interesting death notice in the Statesville, North Carolina, *Landmark*, on October 11, 1884, describes the transfer of "the remains of A. Blum, a Dutch peddler," from Wilmington, North Carolina, to Baltimore. Professor Oscar Handlin, in his book *Adventure in Freedom*, writes that in early New England, too, the Jewish peddler was "looked upon as just another kind of a German." In 1839 there were twenty German Jews in Cleveland, Ohio, who were suddenly confronted with a problem. A Jewish peddler had died. So the twenty Jews bought a burial ground, which united them into a congregation and a community.

The term "Jew peddler" appeared in public print in the early part of this century; later came the term "Jew store," which is still widely used among the rural white and black populations of the South, although it is never intended as an insult. "Is this a Jew store?" asks a black, and the Jewish proprietor, not recognizing the naïveté of the customer, replies: "Yes, this is a Jew store for niggers." Their interest in asking whether this is a Jew store is prompted by a widespread legend that a Jewish merchant will make every possible concession or sacrifice to chalk up the first sale of the day, accepting any offer rather than lose his first customer. The farmers and sharecroppers vie with one another to be the first one in the store to get the "bargain."

Collections were good. The women always had the money for the peddler, who learned that even when on rare occasions they moved away, they caught up with him somewhere to pay him. In those days the black women did not buy any frills or luxuries of any kind, except a gold-filled brooch. The peddlers sold many hundreds of these. The women wore them on Sundays when they went to church. The fleur-de-lis design was the most popular. They sold gold wedding bands to many black women. These cost $10, paid at the rate of 25 cents a week. Clocks were popular. They bought one of two models, the "half-hour strike" or the "banjo type." The price was $8, and the installments were also 25 cents a week.

Business improved for a peddler when he got a horse and wagon. His white customers bought the notions, and sometimes the luxury items for the children, also the ribbon and more particularly the goods by the yard, but the black women bought mostly ready-to-wear things. For the black women he had aprons for 40 cents and housedresses at 80 cents, and late in the fall he put on the wagon two dozen winter coats at $7 each, which he sold on credit and always sold out.

The peddler learned a trick after a while that made him most welcome in the home of the black tenant farmer, as well as in the shacks of the "city" black living at the edge of town. The blacks were beginning to come to the towns in 1905. They worked in the tobacco warehouses pulling the vein out of the tobacco leaf. I understand that now this job is done by machinery. What the peddler learned then was to permit the black to try on the hat or the housedress or the coat, and he let their children try on shoes. In those days, the white merchants did not permit blacks to try on any ready-to-wear merchandise. The black could buy goods only by pointing to what he wanted or asking for it, and both he and the merchant did the best they could in fitting him in this way. But it was understood that if a black tried on any of the merchandise, the merchant would lose his white trade. The peddlers were more or less itinerants, and they knew this was the only way they could do business.

They took no chances. They did not offer any of this ready-to-wear apparel to their white customers, so they could never say a black had tried it on. They made sure that there was never the slightest suspicion of this. As a matter of fact, on many occasions the peddler sold to the white farmer and his wife and children and the black tenant farmers and their families at the same time, all standing around his wagon smiling and feeling good. There might be two black women behind his wagon trying on housedresses over the clothes they were wearing, while the white farmer and his wife looked through his tinware and the children handled the ribbons and the few toys he carried.

The people who did the big business with the peddlers in the South were suppliers, or as they were called, "wholesalers," most of whom were up in New York, Philadelphia, and Baltimore—such firms as Finer & Sons and H. B. Claflin, in New York, and the Baltimore Bargain House. A peddler with small capital couldn't go to New York or to Baltimore to get his supplies, as he needed them every week or so. There were various subcontractors, or jobbers who handled merchandise which they bought from the big suppliers in New York, Philadelphia, and Baltimore. There were jobbers in Norfolk, Virginia, and in North Carolina one jobber was in Yanceyville, while another was in Mount Gilead.

The Cones: Plaids and Picassos

THE CONES of Greensboro, North Carolina, are the only Jewish family in the South to have achieved "Our

Crowd" status, with the Schiffs, Warburgs, Guggenheims, and Speyers of New York.

And they made it all in textiles.

Moses and Caesar Cone were peddlers for their father's wholesale grocery business in North Carolina in the 1870's. Their routes took them through the mill towns and to the company stores established by the cotton manufacturers. These journeys taught them that the new textile industry just starting in the South was fragmentized. When their father closed his wholesale grocery, these two young men set about convincing thirty-eight cotton mills to sell them their output of manufactured fabrics. With this guarantee the two Cone brothers started a commission house in New York. As their selling house prospered, the brothers took over some of the faltering mills. From these efforts came the Cone Export and Import Company, which served both as banker and distributor for the South's textile industry. They also helped the South set up its own milling and finishing processes for the cotton it grew. Until the Cone brothers started their business, the Southern mills turned out only a single product, a cheap fabric known as Southern plaid, which sold for about 10 cents a yard. With an orderly system of distribution established by the Cones, the mills were free to experiment with a wide variety of fabrics, and in the process the Cones themselves eventually came to operate more than 500,000 spindles, or about 3 percent of the entire textile industry in the South.

Caesar Cone was vice-president of the American Cotton Manufacturers Association and was prominent in local and state philanthropic work. His son Herman was, in 1940, the incumbent of most of the posts Caesar Cone had held in the mills. Herman Cone was president of the Greensboro Community Chest and of the Greensboro Boy Scout

Council. Another son of Caesar Cone, Caesar Cone, Jr., contributed the funds for the erection of a YMCA for blacks in Greensboro in 1939. During the bank failures in the 1930's, the family of Caesar Cone, in his memory, guaranteed all the accounts in the North Carolina Bank Textiles Branch.

Moses Cone designated a large portion of his estate to be used for the construction of a hospital in Greensboro.

Caesar Cone donated a large sum of money to the Guilford County North Carolina TB Sanitarium.

Concerned with the problems of health, the Cones saw to it that the villages which grew up around their cotton mills had better sanitation arrangements than most other communities. Their interest also extended to school facilities and schooling, including every branch of cultural and domestic art. Nursing and dairying were also supervised by the mill owners.

The sisters of Herman and Caesar Cone, Claribel and Etta, were remarkable women.

Claribel was a physician and took her medical degree at Johns Hopkins University. She later studied mythology at Senckenberg University in Frankfurt, Germany. She was for a time professor of mythology at Women's College in Baltimore. And from 1926 until her death in 1929 she was pathologist in a hospital, Good Samaritan in Baltimore, Maryland.

Claribel Cone also wrote many scientific articles on bacteriology for American and German medical journals. She was a member of the medical faculty of Maryland and also of the Board of Directors of the Women's Civic League and of the Council of Jewish Women.

A primary interest for both Cone sisters, outside the scientific field, was art. During their lifetimes Claribel and

165

her sister, Etta, accumulated one of the finest collections of contemporary art in the United States. They were considerably aided in this collection by their friendship with Gertrude Stein and her brother, Leo Stein, who introduced them to Matisse and Picasso.

The Cones and the Steins had known one another in Baltimore when Gertrude Stein had been a medical student at Johns Hopkins, during the years that Dr. Claribel Cone pursued her research. They resumed their friendship in Paris, where for many years the Cone sisters were members of a group of intellectuals and art lovers who met in Gertrude Stein's apartment once a week. The Cone sisters went to Picasso's studio frequently and each time bought more drawings. They were doubly welcomed by Picasso who was at that time always broke. They won his heart by bringing him the Baltimore *Sun*'s comics. Etta Cone subscribed to the Baltimore *Sun* Sunday edition for Picasso so that he would always have the comics.

But Matisse became their special friend, and they accumulated one of the largest collection of Matisse paintings in the world. Bernard Berenson, the great art connoisseur, suggested that they look in on Cézanne, who thereupon became another favorite of the Cone sisters.

Claribel found when she got to Paris in 1925 that it was becoming easier and easier to bring herself to buy expensive paintings. At the end of June she cabled Cone Export in New York: "Bought pictures. Cable me through American Express, Paris, twenty thousand in dollars. Claribel Cone, Hotel Lutetia." She then noted the wording of the cable and its cost, 86 francs, in her little notebook and went off again to look long at her newest acquisition. It was a late Cézanne of the artist's favorite scene, Mont Ste. Victoire. Claribel had bought it from Bernheim-Jeune for 410,000 francs—about $18,000—much more than she or Etta had ever paid for any painting in their collection. Before Claribel picked it up on July 1, she used to go to the Louvre to examine the Cézannes through opera glasses.

An interesting incident took place at an auction in Paris where Matisse was startled to discover himself bidding against Dr. Claribel Cone for "The Blue Nude," the Matisse masterpiece. The situation demanded the ultimate courtesy, and Henri dropped out of the bidding. He noted wryly to himself that Dr. Claribel finally bought the picture at a price higher than she would have paid for it, if she had bought it through him in America. The very notoriety of "The Blue Nude" served to characterize its third owner as an art collector of considerable daring. Although the painting was already twenty years old, and although it had hung first in the Stein studio and then in John Quinn's home for a number of years, it was considered the classic horror of horrors known as modern art. Most American collectors were reluctant to buy any nude in 1926, much less "The Blue Nude." Dr. Claribel paid 101,000 francs for the painting. She could hardly wait to see the painting in her living room, and she could hardly wait to show Baltimoreans that naked lady. Etta was somewhat dazed, but in her eyes the master could do no wrong. "The Blue Nude" was a classic, and that was that.

The Cone collection continued to grow. By early 1929 the sisters owned a few dozen Matisse oils and more than a dozen bronzes, innumerable drawings by Etta's favorite artist, Matisse, a fine collection of Picassos, Renoirs, and Van Goghs, as well as their large collections of fabrics and laces. Claribel found herself wondering what they would eventually do with all this. Etta could not bear to think of death or dying, but Claribel realized that it must be faced.

She was ready to face it. She took a long look around her—at the city where she had grown up, where she had become a doctor and had done her research, where she had founded her own museum, where she had been the object of some attention and occasional ridicule. She thought of all the people she knew who laughed at her, at her collecting, and then she thought about the future. The future belonged not to her and not to those who had alternately ignored or ridiculed her. The future belonged to those who were making it. Certainly the paintings she owned were part of that future. Should she pay Baltimore back in kind and give the paintings to another museum, such as the Metropolitan in New York? Should she leave the collection to her family? They had not shown any particular interest in art—old or new. Although they had always been loyal, that did not guarantee that they would not sell the collection at auction after her death or Etta's. Claribel saw the answer. The one person she could trust was Etta. Etta knew; Etta loved; Etta cared. Yet that was not enough, because Etta was too much given to making outsized heroes of personalities. Claribel must set an ultimate and determining goal for Etta. What was the goal to be? Not to send the pictures to a posh, big-city museum in New York, not to allow the collection to be dispersed by the family or the executors.

Before sailing for Europe, Dr. Claribel drew up her will. The art collections were to be given to her sister Etta upon Claribel's death. The ultimate disposition of the collections was to be of Etta's choosing. She also left $100,000, which was to pass to the museum with the collection.

Claribel and Etta lived quietly in Lausanne, seeing their friends or "business associates," as Claribel referred to them, looking at art, reading art books, shopping for linens and laces, taking walks around the town, taking an

occasional excursion on Lake Leman. Claribel made no
mention of her premonition of death. There was no need to.
In September, soon after brother Fred's arrival, Claribel
caught a slight cold that developed into pneumonia. Within
a week she was dead.

Etta learned that she would have to go on living alone.
All that she had dreaded had happened. But she went right
on living.

Among the many letters of grief Etta received, a few
meant a great deal to her:

October 16, 1929

Miss Cone
Hotel Lutetia
Paris, France

DEAR MISS CONE:

I know the words lose all meaning in the presence of great
emotion but allow me to communicate of my painful shock in
learning by a letter from my family of your sorrow. I am
thinking of your immense grief, knowing as I do of your
attachment to Dr. Cone and being able to guess how much her
rich and distinguished personality could have added to your
enjoyment of life.

Do believe, dear Miss Cone, that I share your grief
profoundly.

Affectionately and devotedly,
HENRI MATISSE

1 Place Charles Felix
Nice

Etta spent $15,000 on a Gauguin oil ("Woman with
Mango"). She had seen the sumptuousness of a Tahitian
woman dressed in a blue robe, holding a pink fruit,
surrounded by a deep yellow background and knew that

she must have it. After the Gauguin oil Claribel bought another Renoir bronze, as well as Picasso's "Study for Family," which he had painted in 1920.

Etta produced a catalogue of her collection in 1934. One hundred and twenty-five plates were reproduced in it including works by Matisse, Picasso, Cézanne, Chirico, Courbet, Monet, Degas, Derain, Despiau, Van Gogh, Kisling, Vlaminck, Laurencin, Maillol, and Manet.

Etta died in 1949, and after her death it was thought necessary to guard the apartment's collection, which the newspapers valued at $3,000,000. A Pinkerton guard was installed.

Etta willed the entire art collection to the Baltimore Museum. Their fellow Baltimoreans had considered the sisters eccentric, if not a little crazy. Now in 1949 the newspapers were comparing their collections with the world's great Matisse collections. The Cone collections contained 43 Matisse oils, 18 drawings, and 113 drawings, as well as most of the master's graphic works. It provides a fifty-two-year chronology of Matisse's development from 1895 to 1947.

According to the terms of Etta Cone's will, the entire collection was left to the Baltimore Museum and the city of Baltimore. Claribel Cone had willed $100,000 cash to the museum to help maintain the collection. Now Etta added $100,000 to it.

Today the Cone wing of the Baltimore Museum of Art contains the most discriminating, as well as one of the most comprehensive, collections of modern art in the world.

Moses Ezekiel

MOSES EZEKIEL entered Virginia Military Institute in 1861 and served in the VMI cadet battalion during the Civil War, rising to the rank of lieutenant. At the close of the war he returned to the institute and was graduated in 1866.

Ezekiel had shown an interest in art from boyhood. His first works of sculpture were a bust of his father and the bust "Cain, or the Offering Rejected." He also had painted. After studying anatomy at the Medical College of Virginia for a year, Ezekiel studied art in Cincinnati, where he produced the statuette "Industry." In 1869 he enrolled at the Royal Academy of Art in Berlin, where he worked under the guidance of Rudolf Siemering and Albert Wolff. During the Franco-Prussian War he was special war correspondent for the New York *Herald*.

The first mark of recognition came in 1872 with the completion of a colossal bust of Washington (now in Cincinnati); on the merits of this work he was admitted to the Berlin Society of Artists. With the bas-relief "Israel" (1873) Ezekiel became the first American to win the Michel Beer Prix de Rome. He made his home in the Italian city for the remainder of his life, although making frequent trips to the United States. A section of the ancient Baths of Diocletian served the sculptor as a studio for more than thirty years.

Ezekiel's works bear evidence of an ardent love for American democracy and freedom, which inspired some of his finest productions.

Among the best known of Ezekiel's several hundred statues, portrait busts, and ideal groups is the unique marble "Religious Liberty," commissioned by the B'nai B'rith for the Centennial Exposition in 1876 and placed permanently in Fairmount Park, Philadelphia. Twelve statues by Ezekiel of great artists of the world occupy the niches about the Corcoran Gallery of Art, Washington, D.C. Ezekiel's bronze of Stonewall Jackson stands in front of the State Capitol at Charleston, West Virginia. Other works by this sculptor include the Thomas Jefferson Monument in Louisville, Kentucky, an equestrian Robert E. Lee at Piedmont, Virginia, a Christopher Columbus for the Columbian Exposition in Chicago, and "Virginia Mourning Her Dead" (1903) presented to the Virginia Military Institute as a memorial to those of Ezekiel's schoolmates who were killed at the Battle of New Market. He also did "The Outlook" for the Confederate cemetery at Johnson's Island, Ohio, and the Confederate monument at the Arlington National Cemetery (1914).

Among his works with religious subjects were: "Adam and Eve," "David," "Queen Esther," "Eve," "Judith," "Christ" (Peabody Institute, Baltimore), and an especially notable "Christ in the Tomb," which was placed in the Chapel for Consolation in the Rue Goujon, Paris. In 1888 he designed the seal of the Jewish Publication Society of America.

Ezekiel executed a number of busts, including Beethoven, Liszt, Longfellow, Shelley, Cardinal Hohenlohe, Lord Sherbrooke (for Westminster Abbey), Isaac M. Wise, and Edgar Allan Poe (his last work).

His works are marked by their keenly realistic style, which borders often on naturalism. "Religious Liberty" is

said to have introduced to American sculptors the new German and Italian methods.

Ezekiel was widely honored for his sculpture and received both Italian and German knighthood.

The Jews of North Carolina

THE FIRST JEWS to enter North Carolina probably came from the island of Barbados in the autumn of 1665. Early religious restrictions, however, and the lagging commercial development of the state made for an exceptionally slow rate of increase in the Jewish population.

Names of individual Jews emerged in the historical records of the last half of the eighteenth century. Aaron Moses was witness to a will in 1740. In 1750 David David successfully petitioned the council for a grant of 180 acres of land at New Hanover. In 1752 David's name appeared on the muster roll of the Wilmington County militia. At Edenton, in 1758, Jacob Franks was allowed a claim of proclamation money. In 1750 and 1760 the name of "the Jew," Mr. Laney, appeared in colonial records for the first time, and it continued to appear until 1784 in numerous business transactions. In 1768 William Levy, of Orange County, is noted among the petitioners to the governor setting forth a list of grievances.

To these Jews of North Carolina full civil and religious equality came slowly. In an election of 1702–03 there is recorded a protest against the returns on the ground that the votes of Jews, as well as those of such other undesirables as strangers, sailors, servants, blacks, and Frenchmen, were counted. The established church of the state required support from all citizens; when the Dissenters came into power, they in turn discriminated against the non-Protestant sects. Thus, although the State Constitution of 1776 granted liberty of conscience, it stated also: "That no person who shall deny the being of God or the truth of the Protestant religion or the Divine Authority either of the Old or New Testament, or who shall hold religious principles incompatible with the freedom and safety of the state, shall be capable of holding any office or place of trust or profit in the Civil Department within this state." This provision was dramatically tested when Jacob Henry, a Jew, elected to the legislature in 1808, was reelected in 1809.

Charlotte, North Carolina

CHARLOTTE, NORTH CAROLINA, has three congregations: the Conservative Temple Israel with 450 members; the Reform Temple Beth El with 300 members; and the newly formed Reform Temple Beth Shalom with about 200 members. Beth Shalom was organized by members who broke away from Temple Beth El, and they represent the Ultra Reform or Classical Reform.

Charlotte is a city of close to 300,000 inhabitants of whom 3,000 are Jews. The Jews, as in the rest of the South, are a single proprietary class. They own retail stores selling soft goods and jewelry, and they are in the professions: medicine, dentistry, and the law. Arthur Goodman, a young lawyer, has served as an elected official, district attorney. Morris Speizman is active in the conservative movement of America and the world. Another large contributor to the United Jewish Appeal and Bonds of Israel is Stanley Kaplan, the owner of a local radio station.

I. D. Blumenthal, previously discussed, is famous as the owner of Wildacres, an interfaith project in the mountains of North Carolina; he has been active in several basic projects, such as the itinerant rabbi and the Jewish Home for the Aged at Winston-Salem.

Another Jewish pioneer in Charlotte was Jay Hirshinger, the first Jew to be elected to the school board and to the library board. He was also a founder of the Hebrew Cemetery and of the first temple in Charlotte which later became Temple Israel. Mrs. Marion Cannon, granddaughter of Jay Hirshinger, is a well-known philanthropist and civic leader of the city today.

The Jews of Charlotte remained silent during the entire black struggle for civil rights. Not that they were not sympathetic, but they feared retaliation from the white community.

The local school board made a start toward desegregation of public schools in accordance with the Supreme Court decisions of 1954 and 1955. Charlotte's very able chief of police at the time, Frank Littlejohn, said: "We'll take this in stride in this city; there'll be no trouble, except maybe at Harding High School" (in a low-income neighborhood where the question of caste is so much more significant). The chief was right in his forecast, and it was not a pleasant sight.

The Jewish Country Club

THE JEWS had been trying to get into one of the Gentile country clubs of Charlotte for a half century—to no avail. Then, one day, Police Chief Frank Littlejohn took the slot machines out of one of the Gentile country clubs; this posed a serious financial problem for the club. The directors met and decided to replace the slot machines with Jews. But it was too late. The Jews were building their own, and the Amity Country Club is now in existence for the Jewish community.

This remains the pattern throughout the South. The Jews are excluded from the social country clubs and the downtown city clubs. It reminds me of another story.

Henderson Belk, an apostle of Billy Graham, came to see me and urged me to become a Christian. I said, "Henderson, you don't allow me in the City Club, where I can only spend an hour a week eating lunch, but you want me in heaven through all eternity. There's no logic in this at all."

Seriously, there is more to this exclusion than meets the eye. Exclusion of the Jewish merchant or businessman from these purely social clubs works as a disadvantage to him.

We are a socially oriented society. The pianist who is to perform a concert in the evening has lunch at the City Club. The members of the City Council and the school board meet there occasionally. A visiting educator delivers a lecture there. The Jewish doctor or lawyer has a chance to compete for his services, which is being denied him. Thus the free enterprise boys are afraid of the competition. And that is why they exclude the Jew.

The Amity Club, however, is ecumenical; its roster includes one Wasp, a Mr. Patterson, and an Oriental, Gerald Li, an architect.

Hebrew Cemetery of Charlotte

THE GRANDDAUGHTER of a Revolutionary patriot, two officers of the Confederacy, and dozens of leading merchants and public figures of this city for the past seventy-five years are buried in the Hebrew Cemetery, which is one of the old landmarks of Charlotte and comprises eleven acres at McCall Street and Oaklawn Avenue.

One of its earliest burial plots holds the remains of Elizabeth Cohen, who died in Charlotte in 1872. The name of her grandfather, Moses Cohen, is memorialized on a monument to Revolutionary War heroes in Monroe. Her father, Aaron Cohen, settled in Charlotte in 1824 and followed his profession of goldsmith.

The writer has ascertained that some of the silver and gold plate and tableware designed and manufactured by Aaron Cohen is still in use by two of the old families of Charlotte. His trademark signature was a colonial hat in the center of a Star of David.

The two Confederate heroes buried in the cemetery are Captain J. Roessler of the 40th North Carolina Infantry and Lewis Leon, who enlisted in a regiment from North Carolina, and settled in Charlotte after his liberation from the Northern army camp where he had been a prisoner of war. Captain Roessler, who had been born in Germany, settled in Charlotte in 1851. He enlisted at the outbreak of the war and was discharged in 1864, after a wound had incapacitated his arm. Both gravestones have been noted with markers by the United Daughters of the Confederacy.

Another grave is that of H. Van Straaton, who was buried in 1878. Van Straaton was an artist, born in Holland, who was brought to Mecklenburg County to paint portraits of the children on one of the large plantations on what is now the Concord Road. His work was greatly admired by many other Southerners whose commissions kept him in this country until, finally, he decided to settle in Charlotte. Upon his death, one of his patrons notified the artist's family in Holland, who expressed the wish that Van Straaton be buried in this community and according to the rites of his Jewish faith.

Another pioneer to this community was Simeon Frankford, who first settled in Albemarle and spent many years in Charlotte. He was one of the leaders in the state in Masonry and was well known in the community for his philanthropy among the poor. The cemetery also has a Baruch plot. Rowland Baruch, brother of Dr. Simon Baruch of Camden, operated a dry goods business in Charlotte, and two of his children, Lizzie and Bernard, are buried here. These children would be first cousins of the elder statesman of America, Bernard M. Baruch.

The Hebrew Cemetery is one of the most interesting landmarks of Charlotte. It was first used in 1859 and officially incorporated as the Hebrew Benevolent Society in 1867. The original incorporators were H. M. Phelps, H. Buxbaum, J. Buxbaum, H. Baumgartner, and Jay Hirshinger. In the early part of this century, upon the death of the last surviving incorporator, Mr. Baumgartner, the trusteeship was placed in the hands of Will Weill, who was the president until the society was reconstituted as the

Hebrew Cemetery Association, with M. B. Smith as president, which post he held on behalf of the Jewish community in Charlotte until his death, when the trustee-ship was placed in the hands of his son, Alfred E. Smith, who is now president of the organization.

Gertrude Weil of Goldsboro, North Carolina

GOLDSBORO is a small city in eastern North Carolina, and its most famous store is Weil Brothers. Herman Weil emigrated to the United States from Bavaria in 1858 at the age of sixteen. He first went to Baltimore, where his sisters lived, and then the same year he came to Goldsboro and started peddling. His brother Henry also peddled at one time or another. He finally went into the business, opening a store, but their enterprise was interrupted by the outbreak of the Civil War.

Although he had only a limited knowledge of the English language, Herman Weil was among the first to join Captain J. B. Whitaker's company of Goldsboro volunteers, enlisting on June 28, 1861. Herman was one of the more than 10,000 Jews who served in the Confederate Army. "It was simply a sense of loyalty to their homes and to their neighbors that prompted him to fight for the South," wrote M. Smith, the contractor in firearms for the Army and Navy departments. After the end of the war, Herman and his brother Henry went into business for themselves in June, 1865. In 1866, Herman and Henry were joined by their brother Solomon, age seventeen.

That the Weils were able to make a go of it attested not only to their determination and ability, but also to the esteem in which they were held by the public, for they had quickly established a reputation for honesty and fair dealing.

Writing of the Weil brothers two decades later, Joseph E. Robinson, editor of the Goldsboro *Daily Argus*, said:

> People like these, people of high character and strict personal integrity, are wanted in every community, for upon such men and their wholesome influence depends the safety, the stability and the advancement of the city that possesses them, the state and even the nation.
>
> In the bleak aftermath of a ruinous war, it is understandable that a community welcomed newcomers like the Weils who would put their shoulders to the wheel and help get the economy moving again.

Gertrude Weil was the daughter of Henry and his wife, Mina Rosenthal Weil. I first met Gertrude Weil when we were both campaigning for Dr. Frank P. Graham for the United States Senate. She was the organizer and first president of the North Carolina League of Women Voters.

Chancellor House of the University of North Carolina noted that "For many years Miss Weil has been actively supporting the Women's College of North Carolina at Greensboro. Its present high level is due in no small part to her devotion to high standards of womanhood."

Gertrude Weil served in many capacities among state and local levels.

The women's clubs did a lot in those days. They worked for such things as beautification, improving the schools, and health. Miss Weil did Red Cross work in both wars. In 1953 she was named Goldsboro's Woman of the Year. She almost didn't show up for the award. "It was Friday night, I would have attended services in the synagogue if a club member hadn't told me that I had to be present." She was in the synagogue every Friday night, as well as Saturday morning at the Temple Oheb Sholom. With only thirty-five Jewish families in Goldsboro, attendance at these services was very small, and on one Saturday morning, Miss Weil sat through the service alone. The then Rabbi Julius Mayerberg conducted the entire service for her, including the sermon.

Gertrude's initiation into social service came when she returned home after graduating from Smith College. She was twenty-one at the time. "I planned to be a kindergarten teacher, but my mother was feeble, and I found some social work to do. Miss Mary Arrington had taught me embroidery, and I opened a little sewing class on Edmundson Hill. It was a valuable experience. It was worth a great deal to know how the poor lived."

In 1964, the first year it was offered, Miss Weil was one of the five graduates of Smith College to receive the Smith Medal from her alma mater. The citation read:

> The first from your native North Carolina to graduate from Smith, you returned home to embark on a lifetime of service to the cultural, charitable, religious and political welfare of your state. In their range of significance your efforts to provide a better life for your fellows dramatically illustrate the close connection between the emancipation of women and the progress of our country. The Women's Suffrage League of half a century ago and today's bi-racial council have shared a common concern for equal rights and human freedom, as well as your brave heart, generous spirit and high responsibility. Smith College hopes it can claim some small part of this magnificent accomplishment.

The thirty-five Jewish families in Goldsboro represent a single proprietary class of retailers, salesmen, real estate operators and the construction businessmen. Robert Kadis is head of the United Jewish Appeal, and there's one Jewish doctor, Dr. Trachtenberg.

Miss Weil died at the age of ninety-two in a house not far from the house in which she was born in Goldsboro, where she spent all her years.

Judah Touro

IN A NEWPORT CEMETERY is the tombstone of Judah Touro inscribed: "By righteousness and integrity he collected his wealth; in charity and for salvation dispensed it. The last of his name, he inscribed it in the book of philanthropy, to be remembered forever."

Judah Touro was born the day before the Battle of Bunker Hill, 1775. He was the son of the rabbi of Newport, Isaac Touro, and Reyna Hays Touro.

His father, Rabbi Isaac Touro, lost his position as Newport's rabbi because the War for Independence destroyed Newport's commercial supremacy. Rabbi Touro went to New York, and unable to secure a pulpit, he sailed for Kingston, Jamaica, in 1783. He died there.

His mother's brother, Moses Michael Hays, prominent merchant of Boston, brought the family to Boston. There Judah was educated for business. At twenty-seven Judah decided to embark on a business career independently. In October, 1801, he sailed from Boston to New Orleans. He had selected New Orleans and opened a store there. There were virtually no Jews in New Orleans at this time. He became acquainted with two Virginians, James H. Shepard and Regin Davis Shepard.

Judah Touro and Regin Shepard volunteered in the War of 1812. They were in an engagement under General Jackson at the defense of New Orleans. In the battle Touro was wounded and left for dead. Regin Shepard carried him from the battlefield and nursed him back to health. Touro never forgot that kindness. Shepard was his lifelong friend and one of the four executors of his will and the one to whom he left the residue of his estate, after special bequests.

When General Jackson defended New Orleans in January, 1815, he was unaware of the Treaty of Ghent that had ended the War of 1812 in December, 1814. Communications were meager in those days.

Judah Touro's role in this battle is described by James Barton in his *Life of Jackson*. He writes:

> When the state was invaded Mr. Touro was attached to a regiment of Louisiana militia. . . . After performing severe labors as a common soldier in the ranks, Mr. Touro on the 1st of January, volunteered his services to aid in carrying shot and shell from the magazine to Hemphrey's Battery. In this humble but perilous duty he was seen actively engaged during the terrible cannonade with which the British opened the day, regardless of the cloud of iron missiles which flew around him, and which made many of the stoutest hearted cling closely to the embankment or seek some shelter. But in the discharge of duty, this good man knew no fear and perceived no danger. It was while thus engaged that he was struck in the thigh by a twelve pound shot which produced a ghastly and dangerous wound.

Amos Lawrence of Boston pledged $10,000 for Bunker Hill Monument if any person could be found to contribute a like amount. Touro contributed the $10,000. A banquet was held in Faneuil Hall in Boston on June 13, 1843, to honor Amos Lawrence and Judah Touro, and President

John Tyler attended. Daniel Webster was the orator. Governor Marton wrote a poem for the occasion which was widely circulated:

> Amos and Judah, venerated names,
> Patriarch and Prophet press their equal claims,
> Like generous coursers running neck and neck,
> Each aids the work by giving it a check.
> Christian and Jew, they carry out one plan,
> For though of different faiths, each is in heart, a MAN.

Clapp in his autobiography writes of Touro:

> The most delicate, deserved and timely expressions of esteem from particular, intimate friends and acquaintances, seemed to give him pain instead of pleasure. Mr. Touro once said, in my hearing, that he would have revoked the donations given for completing Bunker Hill Monument, on account of their publishing his name in the newspapers, contrary to his wishes, had it not been for the apprehension that his real motives would have been misunderstood and misrepresented.

When a Universalist church in New Orleans was sold at auction because of the foreclosure of the mortgage, Touro bought the mortgage and made a gift of it to the church.

In 1850 he bought a church and dedicated it as a synagogue. It was called Congregation of the Dispersed of Judah.

In 1852 he bought the Paulding estate, converted it into a hospital, and in his will gave it to the city. The Touro Infirmary still stands as a monument to his kindness.

He lived in New Orleans for fifty years. People set their watches by his comings and goings.

He died in 1854 and left bequests to practically every charitable organization in America. Touro Park in Newport stands near the Old Stone Mill left by the Norsemen and presented by Touro to Newport. Streets in Newport and New Orleans are named in his honor.

"Man looketh upon the outward appearance, but the Lord looketh upon the heart," is the way the Good Book has it written.

Jews in the Battle of New Orleans

Two JEWS had settled in New Orleans by the time of the battle that saved the city from capture by the British. One of these two was Manis Jacobs. An obituary at the time of his death in 1839 said that he had lived in the city for thirty years, but the earliest reference to him is a newspaper advertisement of 1812. The other person unmentioned thus far was Simon M. Cohen. These two round out to fifteen the number of Jewish men definitely known to have been in New Orleans by 1814–15. Of these, at least ten and possibly eleven served in the armed forces under Andrew Jackson on the fields of Chalmette Plantation on January 8, 1815. Two-thirds of any group is a large proportion, but it is important to recall that all these Jews were comparatively young men, some of them single, who were not only willing but able to take part in the defense of their new home.

The records of the military units which took part in the campaign, particularly the home guard, the Louisiana Militia, are scanty and incomplete. In addition to Touro, whose service I have already noted, a contemporary roster, dated December 20, 1814, lists four Jewish men: S. Cohn, a member of the Compagnie des Dragons, Plauche's Battalion of the Louisiana Militia; another "Cohn," who served in the Compagnie des Carabiniers, and who is probably to be identified with Samuel Kohn; Maurice Barnett, listed as a Dragon in the Compagnie des Francs; and J. Hart, of the Compagnie des Dragons (à pied). These are the only early references to military service by Jews which we have been able to uncover.

With a number of men named Jacob Hart in New Orleans at the same time, two of whom were known to be military figures and the third a policeman, it would be difficult to state with any assurance that it was our Jacob Hart who served as a private in Plauche's Battalion, were it not for a list which was published at the time of the thirty-fourth anniversary celebration of the Battle of New Orleans, on January 8, 1849, designating those who were still known to be living at the time. So far as we know, our Jacob Hart was the only man bearing that name who was still alive and in residence in New Orleans—he did not die until December of that year. Another name on that list was Maurice Barnett's. When he died in 1865, an obituary in the *Picayune* said of him: "A veteran gone. We are once again called on to announce the demise of one of the small but highly honored class of our old citizens, the veterans of the Battle of New Orleans, so few of whom remain to us. Mr. Maurice Barnett, Sr. died yesterday. . . ."

New Orleans, Louisiana

RABBI NATHAN SHARE of the Gates of Prayer Congregation told me that there is a great deal of mixed marriage in New Orleans, both involving the conversion of the non-Jewish partner and without conversion. How did the rabbis feel about it? Said Rabbi Share:

"Naturally, we all oppose it and deplore it to varying degrees, but many of us have come to terms with it in one way or another. The Orthodox still take a strong stand against mixed marriage, and their requirements for conversion are quite strict. The Reform rabbis do marry Jews to unconverted Gentiles, but each has his own requirements, and I could not say that what one rabbi would do in a certain case, all of us would do. In my own case, I will officiate if the Jewish partner is a member of my congregation, or has grown up in it, and if the non-Jewish partner will agree to keeping a Jewish home and raising the children as Jews."

The Jewish Welfare Fund of New Orleans raised the sum of $1,300,688 in 1972. Of this, between 65 and 70 percent was for the United Jewish Appeal.

The local Israel Bond office said that in 1973 it had sold over $500,000 worth of bonds.

Some of the leading figures in New Orleans are: Harold Salmonn, Jr., Frank Friedler, Jr., Rene Lehmann, John Weinstein and Martin L. C. Feldman.

The population of New Orleans is 565,000. We estimate the Jewish population to be 10,000 or 12,000.

There is one Jewish country club, the Lakewood Country Club.

I don't know of any Jews belonging to Gentile country clubs in New Orleans, and I have the impression that some of them at least do not admit Jews. Those Jews who have the means and also who have social relationships with each other join the Lakewood club. The poorer Jews play golf on the public courses.

New Orleans Jewry is made up of a mixture of Jews of

German and East European descent. The Germans were here before the East Europeans, a large number of whom came here from 1880 until 1920, and so the Germans (or their descendants who seem to have forgotten the distinction) tend to set the tone in the community. In reality, however, the division in the community no longer is a German-East European one, but rather Reform-Orthodox. Most of the descendants of the German immigrants, naturally, belong to Reform congregations. As the descendants of the East Europeans prosper, many of them move into the Reform circle too.

The general attitude of New Orleans Jewry toward Israel is a strongly positive one.

Busing has not been a problem in New Orleans. As far as I know, there is no busing to achieve "racial balance" here. Attempts to promote integration of the schools have taken other forms, such as trying to place black and white teachers in schools on a 50-50 basis, and so on. Perhaps one of the important reasons why Jews have shown little organized concern over the school problem is that many of them send their children to private schools or have moved to white suburbs.

From a formerly anti-Zionist community, New Orleans has changed into a very positive attitude community toward Israel. Sons of the highly assimilated families have taken a leading part in the Federation, such as Harold Salmon, Jr., who is president of the Jewish Welfare Federation, and Frank Friedler, Jr., who is a former president of the Federation and campaign manager, both of whom have done a good job. Other prominent Jews in Federation work include Mrs. Joseph Cohen, Mr. and Mrs. Herbert Garon, Moise Steeg, Jr., and Mrs. Joseph Bernstein. You should also know that Label Katz, former

international president of B'nai B'rith, comes from New
Orleans. Mrs. Beryl Wolfson, J. Buring, Dave Herman,
Marvin Jacobs, Irving Gerson.

The Jewish enrollment at the universities—and there are
three major universities: Tulane, and the Women's College,
Sophie Newcomb, of Tulane University; Loyola, which is a
Catholic college; and Louisiana State University at New
Orleans—is approximately 1,000 Jewish students going to
these three universities, who are out of city, out of state, and
local.

New Orleans is the only city in America that has a
majority of German Reform Jews and has had for many
years. It is also a community that didn't grow greatly and,
therefore, lived within itself. Like with German Jews, there
was tremendous institutional development and a great deal
of anti-Israel sentiment. All that has changed since 1948. It
is an old community, and in the Reform community, there
are Jews that go back six generations—one family traces its
lineage to Haym Salomon. They are a community that is
one generation ahead of all the other communities in the
United States in age and temperament. Once they were one
generation ahead of the United States in intermarriage, but
this is no longer true. The rest of the country has caught up
to them. Because of the highly social and economic mobility
in New Orleans, and because Jews and Christians had more
contact when the rabbi came here twenty-five years ago,
there was a great amount of intermarriage. There still is,
but in the earliest days, it was probably the tops in
America; today, it's the average percentage with that of the
rest of America. This is not to say that there isn't
anti-Semitism in New Orleans. There is. And there are also
social clubs and Mardi Gras clubs that exclude the Jews,
and this hurts them deeply. Some very wealthy Jews leave

the city during Mardi Gras so as not to be embarrassed by Christian friends who want to come and visit Mardi Gras clubs, to which some of them, Jews, are not invited.

Rabbi Share reports that there is still a good deal of mixed marriages in New Orleans, and there was when the rabbi came there twenty-five years ago because of the social and economic mobility of the Jews. However, he hastens to add that they have gained as many converts in the Jewish community as they have performed mixed marriages. In his own congregation, he has a conversion class for non-Jews and, in some years, he has had as many as two dozen, and most years he averages almost one dozen. When the rabbi came here twenty-five years ago, one out of every six marriages performed was a mixed marriage, and what it is today nobody really knows. In order to survive, Reform rabbis have to perform mixed marriages. Rabbi Share didn't when he first came here, but he found himself losing a part of his congregation, so in self-protection, he had to succumb. He is not happy about it in the sense that the Jewish humanistic rabbis will tell you that they will marry anybody gladly, but the rabbis are facing reality insofar as they would rather have them come to them than go to a secular authority. Intermarriage undoubtedly has increased in New Orleans, as it has increased elsewhere in the United States, especially on the campus, but it has made no inroads, to any extent, in the Jewish community and those Jews who have been connected with the Jewish community.

They are deeply involved in philanthropy, and secular and cultural Judaism, but very little interested in religious Judaism.

The extent of intermarriage during the early years is yet another point of reference from which we can measure the distance of their drift away from Judaism. Of the fifteen Jews who established permanent residence in New Orleans between 1802 and 1815, seven remained bachelors, seven intermarried, and one, Manis Jacobs, married a Christian woman after his first, Jewish, wife died. There is no evidence that any one of the bachelors remained single because he would not marry a Christian. Even after larger numbers of Jews, including whole families, arrived in New Orleans, a high degree of intermarriage continued, probably as much as 50 percent, well into the 1830's.

While it is sometimes suggested that intermarriage leads to the disintegration of Jewish loyalties, it is more likely, at least in New Orleans' experience, that the decision to settle in Louisiana, and therefore to marry a Christian, stemmed from a weakening of consciousness of Jewish identity. These men had already, to some degree, abandoned their Jewish nature and become secularized.

Practically all the children of these intermarriages, as we have seen, were reared as Christians. Alexander Phillips had two daughters who married Jews, but it is not known whether they considered themselves Jewesses. Their feelings may have been similar to those of Maurice Barnett's daughter Helene, who married Sol Audler, but who had her children baptized in the St. Louis Church and was buried in the same Catholic cemetery as her mother. While it is true that there was not a Jewish girl within hundreds of miles of New Orleans whom one of these men might have married, it is at least equally significant that none of them seems to have made any effort to preserve his children from absorption into the Christian population. Although in some cases there was a delay of a few years, baptism was the inevitable rule. The fathers were just not interested in bearing any responsibility for the perpetuation of Judaism.

The extent of intermarriage was not lost on Jacob Solis; when he and his co-workers drew up the constitution and bylaws of the congregation, they broke every Jewish law in their formulation of rules and regulations which concerned "strange" wives and the children of intermarriages. To have forbidden intermarried men from joining the congregation or contributing to it, to have refused any recognition of Christian wives or unconverted children of Christian mothers, would have been tantamount to rejecting a large proportion of the Jews in town. As it was, they need not have worried; many of the intermarried men would have nothing to do with the congregation. None of their children, even Manis Jacobs', identified themselves as practicing members of the community.

Yet it is equally important to emphasize the fact that of all the men who married Christian women, only one, Victor Souza, formally abandoned Judaism and adopted Christianity. All the others, with the exception of Simon Cohen, remained what they were, secularized Jews, unaffiliated Jews, estranged Jews, but still Jews. Some were buried with Christian rites, but not because they had become Christians—this was the decision of their families. Perhaps it was pride, perhaps some primitive feeling of stiff-neckedness that made them resist baptism. But if they had wanted to become Christians, to endure the indignity of adopting a religion which was meaningless to them, in order to secure acceptance by their neighbors, if they had wanted to pay the price of baptism for the "ticket" of admission to Western culture, as Heinrich Heine called it, they could have done that in Europe. Perhaps many another might have sent the message back home, which Dr. Gerson Adersbach did, in his will, that despite everything, he "died without quitting the religion into which he had been born."

The South and Organized Labor

WHEN I SEE a Southern cotton mill worker going to work in an automobile and his wife with a washing machine on her porch, I always think how little they know how much they owe to the Jewish immigrant of the early part of this century—the Jews who were in the forefront of the labor movement in America.

When the teacher asked the kid, "What does your father do?" the young boy answered, "My father's a striker." Everybody was a striker in those days.

The South is today uniformly against labor unions, and every state has a "right to work" law, which is really the right not to have a union shop. The resistance to trade unionism is based on racial segregation. The big argument against trade unionism has always been "Do you want a Negro to work beside you?" It was the big fear, and the employers exploited that fear.

Many of the sewing shops have come South in recent years to escape the labor unions of Seventh Avenue. The Southern states give them many concessions, including no taxes for a year or two, and in some cases the factory is granted free electricity and free water and a free parking lot. The International Ladies Garment Workers Union has tried to organize these factories with little success.

In the first place you can hardly find them. They use different names. One firm in Alabama calls itself Balance Agriculture with Industry, Inc. It makes brassieres.

The Jews of the South reflect the attitude of their neighbors against labor unions. One night I was in a rabbi's house when a young man knocked on the door, said he was a newcomer to the city and wanted to know where in Charlotte he could get a room to stay for a few weeks. The president of the temple was there that evening, and he asked the young man certain questions. How long would he stay in Charlotte, did he have a wife and children? etc. Then he asked him what he did for a living, and the young man answered, "I am an organizer for the textile union." The president of the temple folded his book up and left the room. It was as though a grand inquisitor had entered instead of a young union man.

Dr. Joseph Goldberger and Pellagra

BECAUSE of an immigrant Jew from Hungary, Dr. Joseph Goldberger, millions of Southern children grow up with straight legs and in good health. He was brought to New York City at the age of six. He studied at the College of the City of New York intending to become a mining engineer, but a lecture on a medical subject which he heard by chance swerved him to study medicine and to graduate from college in 1895. For two years he was resident at Bellevue; for two years more he practiced medicine in Wilkes Barre, Pennsylvania.

In 1899, Dr. Goldberger entered the United States Public Health Service. His early work was in tropical and other contagious and infectious diseases. He proved that it was possible to contract malaria more than once. He investigated typhus and almost died of it himself. One of his most spectacular, if minor, achievements was the isolation, within forty-eight hours after he had come on the scene, of the crystalline mite which caused straw itch—a rash that harassed the United States Navy men who slept on straw mattresses.

Even in the first years of his pathological research, Goldberger's approach was unorthodox. Instead of surrounding himself at once with a welter of test tubes, he preferred direct impact with the disease in the environment in which it was rampant. Then his mind was left free to register conditions that would have been blocked off by laboratory procedure.

When he was sent to the southern part of the United States in 1914 to investigate pellagra, Goldberger did not change his methods. Pellagra had been recognized in the United States about that time, but in all likelihood it had been taking a large toll among the black and poor-white populations of the South for many years. Skin discoloration, debility, insanity, and death were its processes. Spain and France knew the disease. The general attitude there, as well as among medical men in America, was that it was contagious or infectious.

Making his usual survey of the surroundings, Goldberger saw at once that those who suffered from pellagra ate different food from those who did not. The pellagrins ate the food they could afford to buy; the healthy groups ate food the pellagrins could not afford to buy. Milk, meat, and greens were included in the diet of the healthy; cornmeal mush, sweet potatoes, and syrup were the food of the pellagrins. Doctors and nurses who lived in pellagra wards in hospitals never acquired the disease, despite the possibilities of contagion and infection.

Goldberger obtained the cooperation of several orphan asylums as experimental stations. The United States government paid for fresh meat and milk, which were fed to children suffering from pellagra. The disease was overcome. Next, Goldberger experimented with twelve volunteers from Rankin Prison Farm in Mississippi. For six months they were kept under strict hygienic observation and fed first-quality food, consisting entirely of syrup, coffee, sugar, cornbread, and sweet potatoes—the characteristic diet of the poor classes of the South. The men passed from good health into a state of debility, then agony. Finally the first skin markings of pellagra appeared.

Medical groups still doubted Goldberger's findings, and he resorted to the most drastic experiment of all. First he, then an assistant, injected the blood of a pellagrin into their own veins. Nothing happened. Several weeks later Goldberger, his wife and several of his co-workers ate a mixture containing the urine, feces, and skin scrapings of a pellagrin. No one contracted pellagra. Here was definite proof that pellagra was not infectious.

Accidentally, during a secondary experiment with dogs, Goldberger discovered that yeast cured pellagra. With the cooperation of William de Kleine of the American Red Cross, yeast was distributed daily in a Southern section chosen for the experiment. Pellagrins were literally brought back to health from their deathbeds. Even after Goldberger's death, since his specific findings about a preventive diet could not yet be put into practice everywhere, the yeast cure still had to be employed. In Sunflower County, Mississippi, there were 1,313 cases of pellagra in 1931. The following year, after 890 pounds of yeast had been distributed, there were only 331 cases.

But Goldberger demonstrated that yeast was only a cure, not a preventive. Once cured, the pellagrins were apt to tire of the ill-tasting medicine and to contract the disease again. Knowing that the proper foods, containing a large percentage of protein, could prevent pellagra, Goldberger strove to evolve a scheme of gardening, whereby the impoverished classes could grow the foods that would secure their immunity. His experiments showed that kale, collards, mustard greens, green cabbage, tomatoes, and turnip greens could be raised easily in small truck gardens.

Ten years elapsed between Goldberger's first researches in the pellagra territory in 1914 and the discovery of yeast as a cure. The successful institution of a planting system that would provide the proper foods is taking a longer time. Between 1928 and 1935 some Southern states showed a 74 percent decrease in pellagra as the result of the increased planting of the necessary greens. In the South as a whole, a 60 percent decrease resulted during the same period.

Goldberger's own explanation of his success was that for two centuries pellagra had been in the hands of the school of impressionistic research, which to him was the school of the researcher who turned in his chair, stared out the window, and then solemnly announced his mature impressions on scientific facts. During the entire reign of the impressionistic school nobody had ever tried the curative effect of diet alone as the sole factor, and Goldberger tried that one simple experiment.

The Strauses

THE STRAUS FAMILY came to the United States from Germany in the middle of the nineteenth century and achieved prominence in merchandising, philanthropy, and diplomacy. The three brothers who first became well known were Isidor, Nathan, and Oscar Straus, the sons of

Lazarus Straus. Lazarus Straus' grandfather, Jacob Lazar Straus, had been a member of the Sanhedrin convened by Napoleon in 1806. Lazarus Straus arrived in the United States early in the 1850's; his wife and sons followed in 1854, settling with him in Talbotton, Georgia. In 1865, following financial reverses resulting from the Civil War, the Straus family went to New York City. In the following year the firm of L. Straus and Sons, merchandising china and glassware, was established, and in 1871, with the leasing by Lazarus Straus of a basement in the R. H. Macy store, for a crockery display, the connection of the family with New York's merchandising life was made.

Isidor Straus, merchant and Congressman, son of Lazarus Straus, was born in Otterberg, Germany, in 1845; he died in the sinking of the *Titanic* off the coast of Newfoundland in 1912. He attended Collinsworth Institute, a high school, and was preparing to enter West Point Military Academy when the Civil War broke out. The Talbotton boys organized a company, of which Isidor was elected first lieutenant, but disbanded when it was found that there was no equipment. He went to London in 1863 as secretary to an agent of the Confederacy who was to purchase a vessel for blockade-running. The trip was unsuccessful, and Isidor stayed abroad for two years, working as a clerk and selling Confederate bonds in Amsterdam and London.

During the Civil War, a wave of anti-Semitism invaded the Southern states for the first time, prompted by misfortunes of the struggle and the need, no doubt, for a convenient scapegoat. Lazarus Straus, who was on good terms with everyone, Gentiles included, in the town of Talbotton, Georgia, was shocked by the appearance of anti-Jewish sentiment in the Southern press. When the grand jury of Talbotton condemned Jewish merchants as evil and unpatriotic, Straus resolved to take his business elsewhere. He moved himself and family and store to Columbus, Georgia, and was even more surprised to discover some of his customers traveling from Talbotton to continue trading at his shop. The story is that he even gained some new customers from Talbotton, who figured if the grand jury says it's bad, it must be good.

Herbert Lehman

HERBERT LEHMAN, four times governor of New York State and United States Senator, was the son of Mayer Lehman, who settled in Montgomery, Alabama, and soon entered the political life of the community. During the Civil War the elder Lehman was associated with the Confederate Army. Jefferson Davis and the governor of Alabama knew him, and he was entrusted with caring for the Alabama prisoners in Northern states. Until this time Lehman, in partnership with his brothers, had been engaged in general merchandising and the cotton business in Montgomery. At the end of the Civil War the family moved to New York, where the banking firm of Lehman Brothers was established by Lehman and his brother Emanuel. In the larger city, too, Lehman was active in communal affairs, Jewish as well as general. He was one of the founders of the New York Cotton Exchange.

When the United States entered the First World War, Herbert Lehman went to Washington to become an aide to Franklin Delano Roosevelt, then Assistant Secretary of the Navy. Later he was commissioned a captain in the Army and assigned to the General Staff in Washington. For his outstanding work he was awarded the Distinguished Service Medal. Lehman retired from active service in 1919 as a colonel of Reserves.

Years before he was identified as an important figure in the political campaigns of Governor Alfred E. Smith, Lehman was well known in Democratic Party circles. As early as 1920 he was one of the staunch and enthusiastic supporters of Smith. In 1924 Governor Smith appointed Lehman to mediate industrial disputes in the garment trades. In 1926 Mayor James J. Walker of New York commissioned Lehman to study the city's finances. He submitted a comprehensive report to Mayor Walker.

Governor Smith appointed Lehman chairman of his campaign committee for the gubernatorial election of 1926, and Lehman served as finance chairman for the Smith Presidential campaign of 1928. During the national campaign Smith, in looking around for men to strengthen his bid for votes in New York State, chose Lehman to run for lieutenant governor with Franklin Delano Roosevelt as the candidate for governor. Roosevelt and Lehman were elected by a small margin, while Smith lost New York State by a large plurality.

Lehman's wide knowledge of business affairs and his years of association with philanthropies and New York's needle trades were valuable assets to the Roosevelt administration. Lehman brought great energy and industry to the job of lieutenant governor, and for the first time the position became valuable in the administration of the state's affairs. Roosevelt delegated many tasks to his lieutenant governor, and they were carried out with precision and thoroughness.

Conversions to Christianity

LIKE THE STORY of the Old South, the history of the Jews within it has been sentimentalized. The sagas of Francis Salvador, Judah P. Benjamin, and Dr. Simon Baruch are as interesting as they are heartwarming, but they represent only a weak link between the South of the Old Plantation Days and the ebb and flow of Jewish life today.

In such cities as Charleston and Sumter (South Carolina) and Columbus and Savannah (Georgia), one still finds on the synagogue rolls a Mendoza, a Laporte, a Moise, or a Kiralfy; but in the main the descendants of the Sephardic Jews who came to Savannah in 1733, and who built a synagogue in Charleston in 1750, have all but disappeared. Some of them live in other parts of the country, but many of them are now third- and fourth-generation Christians.

Oddly enough, formal conversions to Christianity were few and far between even during the second half of the nineteenth century, when Jewish communal life was almost wholly nonexistent. In most cases the family drifted into Christianity through the process of "elimination." The Jew married a Christian; the children were reared as Christians; they in turn married Christians. Through all this the head of the family continued to maintain at least a perfunctory connection with Judaism and the temple, but upon his death the link snapped.

Even in our own day, this process is approaching the inevitable severance with five or six outstanding families in the South. When the head of each of these families passes on, all ties with Judaism and the Jewish community will have come to an end.

The slow Christianization has its own folklore. Every community in the South has at least one leading Protestant layman of whom it is whispered, "He was once a Jew." Even the names have persisted. There are Christians in the South with names like Herschberger, Mordecai, Salomon, Goodman, Hayman, Hertzinger, Rosenblatt, with frequent Baumgardners, Jacobs, and Isaacs. These are the same names you see on the early-nineteenth-century gravestones in the Hebrew cemeteries of Richmond, Charlotte, Charleston, and Savannah. In one Southern town the name of the president of the Hebrew congregation (an immigrant from Poland) was Smith, and the name of the local Lutheran pastor was Kohn.

Jacksonville, Florida

RABBI LEFKOWITZ was in the plush Thunderbird Motel in Jacksonville to preside over one of the lecture sessions for a visiting educational conference. An old-timer with a reputation for humor and goodwill, the rabbi has been in Jacksonville for twenty-eight years and is associated with Temple Ahavath Chesed, of which Israel Kaplan is the ever-popular rabbi emeritus. During the course of an informal afternoon discussion, Rabbi Lefkowitz gave his impressions of problems and prospects facing the Jews of Jacksonville.

What are the big worries for the landsmen of Florida's second largest city? Nothing, it would appear, of any great proportion. The number of Jewish young people involved in drugs or lawbreaking is small. If parents have fears for their children, they concern the rising propaganda for Jesus, which is vigorous in and around the Jacksonville area. Not that anyone expects mass conversions, but youthful rebellion sometimes takes strange forms and manifestations. And the young people these days seem to be searching for answers. They turn to Hare Krishna, Indian mysticism, tarot cards, and the Jews for Jesus movement. Perhaps this interest in "universal answers" is only another fad, and there is no real threat to the parent religion, only a temporary chasing of spiritual butterflies.

On the other hand, there are many signs of promise. Jewish youth in Jacksonville are more conscious of their Judaism than earlier generations: They wear buttons and display bumper stickers about Israel and European Jewry. They are also turning away from profit-oriented careers and seeking work in areas bringing personal satisfaction— research, education, the service professions, environmental and ecological study. Today Jews are represented in the Jacksonville Symphony orchestra, on the judges' benches, and in the City Council. Tomorrow perhaps their impact on the life of the city will be even more pronounced, not only as Jews, but as useful and concerned citizens.

Jacksonville is a city of 500,000, with a Jewish population of 6,000, or about 1¼ percent of the total. Most of the Jewish community live on the south side, though there is no specifically Jewish neighborhood anywhere in the city. There is no flight-to-the-suburbs movement in Jacksonville, though in recent years a small contingent of Jewish families have left the city to settle in the attractive Jacksonville Beach area. Many Jewish kids attend Wolfson High School in South Jacksonville, considered the best academically of the city's high schools. Wolfson's principal grew up in

Brooklyn and is understanding about Jewish holidays and ritual observances.

Jacksonville's Jews are a bit edgy about the liberal causes; like their ancestors down through the ages, they fear to offend the host community, which is largely conservative. For this reason, as well as for others, there was a large proportion for Nixon among the Jewish vote rather than for McGovern. There are, however, no racist Jews in the city on the St. Johns. Some Jewish parents might oppose the busing of public school students, but that is largely based upon a sense of inconvenience. Busing no, but integration yes. Progressive Mayor Hans Tansler set up biracial committees, but outside these meetings black-Jewish relations are minimal. As for interfaith relations, the noon meal is the primary occasion for get-together between Jacksonville's Jews and Gentiles.

Social life for the city's Jewish families revolves around the Beau Clair Country Club, temple functions, and several popular supper clubs. The largest synagogue in Jacksonville is the Conservative Jewish Center, with a membership of approximately 850 families. Orthodox Jews attend Etz Chaim, with a membership of approximately 100 families and is a new offshoot of the Conservative Jewish Center. Reform Temple Ahavath Chesed has about 650 Jewish nembers, whose rabbi is Sidney Lefkowitz. All the rabbis of Jacksonville are working to reduce the large percentage of H_2O Jews in the city at large—H_2O Jews being those members of the congregation who attend temple on Two Holidays Only, Yom Kippur and Rosh Hashonah.

Jacksonville's prosperous Jewish community sponsors numerous service organizations, some of which have been nationally recognized for excellence. The Jewish Community Council is headed by Joel Goldman and directed by Sam Rosenthal. The council conducts an annual Welfare Fund campaign to provide support for the United Jewish Appeal and the Israel Emergency Fund, as well as to fund local organizations. The Jewish Family and Children's Services, under president Bennett Hirsch and director Lawrence Rackow, does family counseling, extends loans, and visits the sick and the imprisoned. It also finds employment for those in need and offers care for the aged. Donald D. Cohn is the new president of River Garden Hebrew Home for the Aged, which provides housing and medical care for the infirm and aged of the Jacksonville community. Since its inception in 1946, River Garden Home has admitted more than 500 residents. River Garden Auxiliary is the largest of Jacksonville's organizations for Jewish women. Presided over by Mrs. Paul J. Witten, the auxiliary sponsors art classes and entertainment for the residents of River Garden Home and generally tries to create a "home atmosphere" that will give the aged a sense that they are not forgotten.

Mount Carmel Gardens, directed by Jack Coleman, is an attractive apartment complex for senior citizens, both Jewish and Gentile. David Goodman heads the Zionist Organization of America, which applies political pressure at home and in Washington to counteract pro-Arab interests. Senior Hadassah, with Mrs. Maurice W. Goldstein as president, sponsors cultural and educational forums and last year conducted a successful fund-raising campaign for medical research. The National Council of Jewish Women is active in Jacksonville, and a B'nai B'rith Lodge has been responsible for a number of services and highly successful programs. A variety of youth organizations offer constructive group activities to Jacksonville's young people.

Some of the city's civic leaders complain that participation in these projects and organizations is spotty and sporadic, that there are 50 or 100 concerned individuals who do all the work and bump into each other at all the meetings. "I see the same faces so often," says one very active community worker, "that last meeting I proposed we all move in and room together."

Nonetheless Jacksonville's record of Jewish service to the community, both Jewish and Gentile, as well as its level of concern for the unfortunate, is an occasion for pride and rejoicing.

Today Jacksonville is North Florida's fastest growing metropolis. As the city expands and prospers, so will its Jewish community—toward more involvement and greater contributions to the welfare of Jacksonville.

Austin, Texas: Judaism in a Nutshell

CHECKING on the Jewish situation in Austin, I found Rabbi Judah Leon Fish of the Agudas Achim Conservative congregation, who is also president of the Kallah of Texas Rabbis. He told me that the rabbis of Austin will officiate at the marriage of two Jews only. If a non-Jew and a Jew want to marry, the rabbi will not perform the ceremony unless the non-Jew converts to Judaism. A number of such marriages take place each year. There are also some marriages celebrated by Christian clergy or by civil officials where the non-Jewish party does not accept Judaism.

The University of Texas at Austin has the largest Hebrew studies program of any state university in the

United States—807 students, with more than 40,000 volumes of Hebraica and Judaica in the library.

There are no Jewish country clubs in Austin. Jews are welcome in several country clubs.

Dr. Marion Stahl is president of the Jewish Community Council of Austin; Dr. Phillip Kocen, president of Congregation Abudas Achim; Sam Shanblum, president of Temple Beth Israel; Mrs. Milton T. Smith (Helen G.) is president-elect of International B'nai B'rith Women; Milton T. Smith, president of B'nai B'rith District Grand Lodge; Mrs. Thomas S. (Min) Friedman, past president, B'nai B'rith Women District Grand Lodge; Mrs. Mannie Solon, past president, BBG International; the late Jim Novy of blessed memory, a close friend of former President Lyndon B. Johnson.

Rabbi Louis Firestein heads the Reform Temple Beth Israel and Rabbi James Lee Kessler is director of the Hillel Foundation at the University of Texas.

Houston, Texas

THE POPULATION of Houston is approximately 1,300,000, and there are 20,000 Jews in Houston. Most of the Jews live in the Meyerland area with many Jews moving into the Memorial area.

There is no reason for Jews to seek membership in Gentile country clubs. The Westwood Country Club has ample space for additional members. In fact, the Westwood Country Club caters kosher dinners if anyone requests it. I would like to add that kosher affairs may be arranged at the

Houston Oaks Hotel and the Marriott Motel, the Sham-
rock, the Sonesta, and the Warwick Hotel, as well as the
Westwood Country Club.

Houston has two kosher meat markets: Goodman's
Kosher Meats, 7215 Stella Link Road, and M & M Kosher
Meat Market, 8532 Stella Link Road. Houston also has a
kosher retail bakery which is called Three Bros. Bakery
located at 4036 South Braeswood.

The Jewish Community Center has a brand-new building which happens to be beautiful. The building cost
between $3,000,000 and $4,000,000.

The United Jewish Appeal raised $3,031,130 in 1972.

The United Jewish Campaign in its emergency fund
raised $1,665,286 to be sent to Israel and also had $608,-
696 allocated to Israel from the regular funds. Hence,
$2,273,982 was to be given by the U.J. Campaign to Israel.
The remaining $757,148 was to remain in Houston and the
United States.

The makeup of Houston Jewry today is primarily
native-born; however, there are still some of the old
generation who were born primarily in Russia, Poland,
Lithuania, and Austria-Hungary.

The general attitude of Houston Jewry toward Israel is a
positive one. In fact, the Beth Israel Reform congregation,
which in 1943 stated as one of its seven principles that it
was not interested in the rebirth of Israel, only last year had
a Bonds for Israel dinner.

At the present time there is only one small congregation,
the Houston Congregation for Reform Judaism, which
probably still has negative attitudes toward the State of
Israel, even though it makes no public pronouncements in
that regard. It would probably be safe to say that its
attitude toward Israel is a neutral one at present. Its rabbi,

Rabbi LeBurkien, however, is pro-Israel and has even spent time in Israel. The Jewish community of Houston, however, each summer sends those who have just completed the eleventh to Israel on a seven-week pilgrimage. Rabbi Segal said: "Approximately forty-five boys and girls have been going for the past few years, and I must state that this will be increased in the years to come. For the summer of 1973 it is estimated that we will have in the vicinity of eighty boys and girls attending our Israeli pilgrimage. In fact, from the letters that I have received this summer and from the youngsters with whom I have talked last year, I can safely conclude that this seven-week Israeli pilgrimage has been the most effective tool that Houston has in regard to perpetuating Judaism for their children."

The president of the Jewish Federation is presently Sol Weiner.

Some of the leading Houston Jews are:

Robert Hecht, past chairman of the United Jewish Campaign.

Sol Weiner, past president of Beth Yeshurun and presently president of the Jewish Federation.

Harold Falik, past president of the U.J. Campaign and past president of the Jewish Community Council.

Gerald Rauch, past president of the United Jewish Campaign and past president of the Jewish Community Council.

Bernard Weingarten, past president of the U.J. Campaign and past president of the Jewish Community Council.

Billy Goldberg, chairman of the 1973 U.J. Campaign and national officer of the B'nai B'rith.

Milton Levit, past president of the Jewish Community Council and past chairman of the U.J. Campaign.

Livingston Kosberg, assistant secretary of the Jewish Community Council and one of the leaders of the U.J. Campaign.

Dr. Leo Horvitz, past president of the Jewish Community Council and president of the Houston Commission on Jewish Education.

There are about 800 Jewish students at the University of Houston, 100 at Rice University, and 31 at St. Thomas University. There are 35 Jewish faculty members at the University of Houston, 4 at Rice. The Jewish faculty members at the University of Houston are well scattered, most of them being in the sciences, education, and the arts.

One nationally known Jewish professor at the University of Houston is Dr. Richard Evans in the Psychology Department, who has written extensively in the field of social psychology and has done many films with the famous psychologists of this age.

At St. Thomas University there is a Jewish professor, Dr. Joseph Goldman, who heads the Institute of Storm Research. St. Thomas also has Rabbi Robert Kahn, of Temple Emanu El, who teaches a course in Jewish history.

If there is any evidence of black anti-Semitism in Houston it is quite minimal. The Anti-Defamation League sometime ago indicated that the stereotype that the Jew owns most of the businesses in the black neighborhood is false.

"Mixed marriages and intermarriages are both problems in Texas, especially in Austin, where the University of Texas is located. In fact, it is a major problem at all campuses. If 'intermarriage' means a Jew marrying someone converted to Judaism, I do not consider that a major problem since a convert to Judaism is, by Jewish law, a Jew. We do have at Beth Yeshurun two classes for aspiring converts. Each class meets on sixteen consecutive Monday evenings from seven to nine P.M. Each convert must submit three study guides (approximately five hundred questions to be completed), submit an essay on the Biblical writings, submit an essay on a contemporary work on a Jewish theme, take a twenty-five-minute oral examination before three rabbis, attend services each week during the sixteen weeks, attend all sixteen sessions of the class, plus a Hebrew test. They have two sessions a year, with an enrollment of approximately fifteen aspiring converts during each session. However, only about forty percent conclude the course since many of them find other places in Houston where conversion is much easier," continued Rabbi Segal.

"The Orthodox rabbis do not perform any intermarriage. None of the Conservative rabbis performs any intermarriage. However, three of the five Reform rabbis who are presently in Houston have performed intermarriages on different occasions. True, some of them have specific rules in regard to the performance of an intermarriage, but intermarriages have been performed by these three. The two other Reform rabbis do not perform intermarriages and have so stated. True, even the three who have performed intermarriages are not in favor of them, but under certain circumstances they do perform them. The Orthodox and Conservative rabbis totally oppose them, and I believe that the two Reform rabbis also unreservedly oppose them."

The young people in Houston with positive attitudes toward Judaism do not want to run away from it. On the contrary, they are interested in helping the Jews in Russia, helping Israel, and working for different Jewish organizations.

Houston has two day schools. One is the Beth Yeshurun Day School with a prenursery, nursery, and kindergarten of

225 students and grades 1 through 6 with 185 students. There is also an Orthodox-oriented day school called the South Texas Hebrew Academy, which will have four grades this year, plus a nursery and kindergarten. This is much smaller than the Beth Yeshurun Day School.

There is also a home for the aged in Houston which is presently full. In the near future it expects to expand.

Rabbi Jack Segal of the Conservative Congregation Beth Yeshurun, who provided this information for me, advises that his organization also sponsors an extremely active adult education program, which not only meets in the fall, winter, spring but during the month of July. Attendance at these programs range from 150 to 1,200.

In addition to the major programs, the rabbi conducts two semesters of seven weeks each on Wednesday evenings, at which time six different lecture classes are presented from 9:15 to 10:15 P.M., and a major presentation with a different local lecturer on a Jewish theme is presented from 8 to 9 P.M. with attendance from 200 to 550 people.

On Monday evenings for thirty sessions they present language courses in Beginner's Hebrew, Intermediate Hebrew, Spoken Hebrew, Introductory Yiddish, and Intermediate Yiddish, as well as in Talmud in English.

Also Beth Yeshurun has a regular Talmud lecture (Shi-ur), as they used to be conducted in the European yeshivas, every Saturday afternoon, at which time approximately twenty-five men and women attend.

Rabbi Segal delivered his Yom Kippur sermon in 1972 on an interesting subject. He told his congregation that practically three out of four Jewish girls in college have had sexual relations by the time she is twenty-two years old.

For twenty-one-year-olds, the percentage he found was

53.6; for twenty-year-olds, 44.7; nineteen-year-olds, 34.3; and eighteen-year-olds, 24.6.

The survey was conducted among 855 Jewish girls at the universities of Houston, Texas, Baylor, Rice, Oklahoma, Tulane (Sophie Newcomb College), Texas A & M, Texas Woman's University, North Texas State University, and St. Thomas University.

The rabbi said his research showed a significant difference in regard to premarital sex between those Jewish girls who had a positive belief in God and devotion to Judaism as against those who held negative beliefs. He added that the difference was also revealed in those who attended services regularly and those who never attended services.

He labeled this difference as the "religious factor," and quoted Dr. Kinsey, who nineteen years ago said: "There appeared to be no other factors which affect the female's pattern of pre-marital behavior as markedly as the decade in which she was born and her religious background."

Rabbi Segal's research occupies 400 pages and 170 tables of statistics. He said that 125,000 bits of information were fed into the computer.

Rabbi Segal offered his congregation these conclusions:

Our children are definitely influenced by the environment in which we live. During the last ten years we have experienced a sexual revolution in the United States—and our daughters, too, have been influenced by that revolution.

Our attachment to our religion definitely affects our premarital sexual behavior. Where there has been minimal attachment to Judaism, there has been greater premarital activity. Where there has been maximal attachment to Judaism, there has been less premarital activity.

David Levy Yulee

THE NAME YULEE is well known in the state of Florida. Before the Civil War David Yulee served in the United States Senate. During the conflict he was a member of the Southern Congress, and after it was over, he became president of the Florida Railway system. He was devoted to the railroads, and during the war he had fought to preserve them from the cannon foundries which demanded them for use in the Cause. For twenty years Yulee promoted the railways and tried to keep them from being scrapped. He eventually persuaded English capitalists to buy out the stockholders.

The fact is, Yulee was born David Levy in 1810 on the island of St. Thomas. His father had bought land in Florida in order to found a Jewish colony there. David broke with his father while still in his teens and wound up in St. Augustine studying law. Thereafter he entered politics and rose by virtue of his heartfelt devotion to the state of Florida. At the age of thirty-six he married the daughter of the ex-governor of Kentucky, who was a celebrated beauty of the time. When he was elected to the Senate, he added a patronymic and we find his name listed as David Levy Yulee.

Charleston

WHEN RHETT BUTLER leaves Scarlett O'Hara at the conclusion of *Gone with the Wind*, he says he might go back to his hometown of Charleston. He says he yearns for things like "roots that go deep . . . the calm dignity life can have when it's lived by gentle folks, the genial grace of days that are gone." For the Jews of this principal city of South Carolina, Charleston also has roots that go deep and pleasant associations of genial, gracious living.

From its earliest days the city of Charleston has been hospitable to Jewish settlers. Its constitution, drafted as early as 1669, specified that all newcomers were entitled to equal rights along with the Anglican citizens who constituted the majority, including "heathens, Jues and other disenters." This openly advertised atmosphere of tolerance attracted a good many Jews, who from that day to this have contributed to the well-being of the picturesque Southern city.

A Spanish-speaking Jew acted as translator for the first governor in his dealings with the Florida Indians. In the eighteenth century, Jews came to Charleston from London, France, Holland, Poland, the Dutch East Indies, and the large cities of the northern United States. In the 1790's they built a temple that was for many years regarded as the handsomest synagogue in America.

One of the most prominent names of the pre-Revolutionary period is that of Moses Lindo, who came from London and settled in South Carolina in 1756. Lindo had something special to offer in the development of the colony—an interest in and a knack for handling indigo, the dye which was derived from certain plants to produce a strong blue tint of great permanence. At the time Lindo was one of the world's chief authorities on the valuable stuff. He had studied at one of the leading scientific schools of London and had performed experiments on his own, which were on record at the Royal Society.

Because of Lindo's work in South Carolina, indigo manufacture and export became one of the chief industries of the colony. By 1754 Charleston was shipping more than 200,000 pounds of indigo, and the amount was to increase to more than 1,000,000 pounds by the year 1775. The colonists needed blue, and Moses Lindo helped supply it.

In 1762 Lindo was appointed inspector general for the province in matters of indigo, drugs, and dyes. The petition for his appointment stated that "because of the services rendered to this province by Mr. Moses Lindo and as a testimonial of his abilities he be made public inspector . . . he is the only person known to us capable of rendering this province public service in that article." Transactions of the Philosophical Society and other records dating from the time reveal Lindo's constant researches and discoveries in his profession. In 1772, ten years after Lindo's appointment, the archives yield a bit of curious and intriguing information: Moses Lindo had resigned his position. The reason? He could not bring disgrace on himself and the colony by certifying inferior indigo. Obviously someone in the industry was cutting the stuff, sending out pale blue to water down South Carolina's reputation in the industry.

Two years later Moses Lindo died.

The golden age of Charleston Jewry came during the period between the Revolutionary and the Civil wars. The Jewish community grew to more than 600 members in this period, and they acquired a reputation for wealth, culture, and solidity almost unparalleled in other cities of the South. In the nineteenth century the Jews of Charleston participated actively in the politics of the city and state, they entered freely into the non-Jewish social life of the community, and they contributed immeasurably to the professional and cultural life of the city, particularly in the areas of literature, medicine, engineering, and architecture. They were also known as people who entertained lavishly and contributed generously to charitable causes.

Members of Charleston's Jewish community served with distinction in the War of 1812, in the Seminole War of 1836, in the Mexican War, and in the Civil War. The prominent Mordecai family contributed many thousands of dollars to the Confederate treasury, as well as provided generous care for untold numbers of destitute Charleston women and children, widowed and orphaned during the conflict. In addition, Charleston Jewry sent so many husbands and sons to fight for the Confederacy that it was virtually impossible to raise a minyan during the years 1862–65.

The Jews of Charleston also played a major role in the religious life of American Jewry in general. In the 1820's a group of restless members resigned from the synagogue and formed their own small congregation to organize the Reform Society of Israelites, which stressed changes in the liturgy and the introduction of English into the services. Thus, these early Charlestonians represent the forefathers of the Reform movement in American Judaism. In the late 1800's the Reform congregation of Charleston introduced such forward-looking measures as a revised prayer book and the admission of women to full membership on the board of trustees. Meanwhile, the Orthodox congregations of Charleston were also thriving and today enjoy a healthy membership.

As a city of 260,000, with about 2,800 Jewish people, Charleston has a beautiful new community center, and the United Jewish Appeal raises about $500,000 a year, of which $90,000 is for Israel, and Charleston buys $300,000 worth of Israel Bonds a year.

Kahal Kadosh Beth Elohim, the temple which gave birth to the Reform movement in America, today is completely true to Israel. All Charleston Jewry is proud of the history of this temple, even though Orthodoxy still has some reservations about Reform.

Prominent Charleston Jews of the twentieth century include the author Octavus Roy Cohen; Samuel Rittenberg, member of South Carolina's General Assembly; Dr. Leon Baney, president of the International Society of Medical Health Officers; and Rabbi Benjamin Axelman.

Father of Jewish Reform

THE FATHER of the Jewish Reform movement, Isaac Harby, was born in Charleston, South Carolina, in 1788. At seventeen he studied law, but pressed by the necessities occasioned by his father's death, he returned to journalism and teaching. He eventually edited the *Quiver* and the *Southern Poet* and contributed to other magazines in the country.

Harby achieved distinction as an essayist and was pronounced the finest literary critic of his day in America. He was the leading spirit of the Reform movement in Judaism organized in Charleston in 1824. In his pioneering of this movement from 1824 to 1833, Harby proposed to abridge the service, to supply the English equivalent of Hebrew passages retained in the services, and to provide sermons in English.

After he removed to New York, he established a school and contributed to the *Evening Post* and other periodicals. Six months later he died at the age of forty. Among his friends and admirers were Thomas Jefferson, James Madison, Edward Livingston, and other distinguished statesmen.

Levi Charles Harby of Charleston

CAPTAIN LEVI C. HARBY of South Carolina had seen action as a youth in the War of 1812, in which he was captured and confined to the infamous Dartmoor Prison. After his release he helped the United States Navy clear the seas of Moslem pirates who robbed American ships. He took part in the Seminole War in Florida and later fought as a volunteer in Mexico.

When the Civil War broke out, Captain Harby was sixty-eight years old, but no matter. The South needed his experience. He was given the command of volunteers on the boat *Neptune* and later distinguished himself in the Battle of Galveston.

Levi Myers Harby

LEVI MYERS HARBY was a brother of Isaac Harby. He entered the United States Navy at an early age, becoming a midshipman, and subsequently rose to the rank of captain, becoming generally known by the name of Captain Levi (or Livi) Charles Harby. During the War of 1812 Harby was taken prisoner by the British and confined at Dartmoor, England, for eighteen months. After his escape, he returned to the United States and continued in the naval service. The year 1836 found him in Texas, aiding the Texans in their struggle for independence. Harby was cashiered from the Navy for having sided with the Texans, but he was reinstated upon the admission of Texas into the Union.

Captain Harby figured in numerous wars. He took part in the Mexican War and in the war against the Seminoles in Florida. He fought against the pirates of Algiers and Tripoli, also in the Bolivian War of Independence. South Carolina having seceded from the Union, Harby espoused the Confederate cause during the Civil War. He distinguished himself in the defense of Galveston and commanded a fleet on the Sabine River. His was an adventurous career, not without romance. In 1838 Harby married Leonara De Lyon of Savannah, Georgia. Mrs. Harby was a Hebrew scholar and taught the first Jewish Sunday school in Texas in 1862.

The Mordecais of North Carolina and a Jewish President of Duke University

THE MORDECAIS were a Southern family who distinguished themselves in law, education, and military affairs over a span of 150 years of American history. The original settler on these shores was Moses Mordecai, who emigrated from Germany to England and finally came to Philadelphia in 1750. His son, Jacob, became a country merchant in the town of Warrenton, North Carolina, and eventually set up the first private school for girls in the South.

The Boarding School for Girls, established in 1809 in Warrenton, educated young ladies of the South for a period of twenty years. All of Jacob Mordecai's seven children taught at the school or assisted in some way. From the beginning they had so many applicants for admission that they had to turn them away. Mrs. Mordecai was Jewish mother to literally thousands of girls, whose affection for her was legendary throughout the South.

Jacob Mordecai's sons studied medicine or law and enjoyed distinguished careers in North Carolina, Alabama, and Virginia. One of Jacob's boys, Alfred, attended West Point, was graduated first in his class, and went on to perform outstanding service for the United States military. In the 1820's he taught at West Point, was commissioned lieutenant, and served thereafter in the Engineer Corps. Later stationed at Washington, Alfred Mordecai became an expert in the use of weapons and was appointed captain of ordnance. So well versed was Mordecai in this area that he wrote the *Ordnance Manual* for the United States Army, the authoritative handbook of its day.

Promoted to brevet major, Mordecai regretfully resigned from the Army at the approach of Civil War in 1861. Sacrificing his hope of advancement, Major Mordecai found it impossible to bear arms against an enemy that might include members of the Mordecai family. He retired to Philadelphia, where he spent his remaining twenty years. In this Indian summer of his life Major Mordecai indulged his interest in reading and scholarship. Even at West Point he had been known as a distinguished student of world literature, devoted to the classics in Latin, French, and English. Now his encyclopedic knowledge became legendary. Often the librarian at the Philadelphia Library would refer questions to Major Mordecai. To the end he carried about with him the odes of Horace in the original Latin. He died in 1887 at the age of eighty-five.

Meanwhile, Major Mordecai's son, Alfred, Jr., had been

graduated from West Point on the eve of the Civil War. He was commissioned second lieutenant of topographical engineers and saw action with General Oliver Otis Howard at the First Battle of Bull Run. Later he was promoted to lieutenant colonel for distinguished service on the field and in the Ordnance Department. Alfred, Jr., became the best-known ordnanceman in the United States Army, served as instructor of gunnery at West Point, and was in command of Watervliet Arsenal. He rose to the rank of brigadier general before his death in 1920.

Thus the Mordecais served their regions and their nation with distinguished service in their various fields of endeavor.

The family was assimilated into Christianity toward the end of the nineteenth century; its most distinguished member of this generation was the late Samuel Fox Mordecai, for many years dean of the Trinity College (later Duke University) Law School. Reared in the Christian religion from birth, he had once been mentioned for the position of president of Trinity College. Dean Mordecai wrote a humorous sonnet, "Trinity's Jewish President":

> With trite constructive platitude,
>   I now express my gratitude
> To each and every person who
>   heard my 'naug'ral through;
> And I'm sure that my election
>   Shows great powers of selection
> In those who chose for President
>   Mr. Mordecai, the Jew.

The Mordecais of Charleston

BENJAMIN MORDECAI of Charleston contributed $10,000 to the Confederate cause as soon as South Carolina seceded. He also organized the Free Market of Charleston, which supported some 600 families in distress during the height of the war. He was also a generous donor to the Home for Widows and Orphans of fallen soldiers and had such faith in the Southern Cause that he invested all his money in Confederate bonds. His enthusiasm got him into trouble later, for as a trustee he sank trust funds into the Southern Cause. Later the beneficiary filed suit against Mordecai and won, the judge offering the opinion that the trustee had no business "risking to the chances of the whirlpool" money entrusted to his care.

Moses Cohen Mordecai of Charleston was a well-known merchant and public figure. He served two terms as state senator from his district. He devoted two ships to the hazardous business of blockade-running and by the end of the war was penniless. With his son, Moses Mordecai moved to Baltimore and became agent at large for a number of steamship companies. By 1870 he had done well enough to continue his charities on behalf of his home state. Claiming the bodies of dozens of Confederate soldiers who had fallen in battle, Moses Mordecai had them transported back to their homes at his own expense.

Jews of the South and the Civil Rights Movement

IN THE NORTH the Jewish immigrant had to wait till his children had become Americanized before there was a chance for the family to enter the open society. But Protestant Fundamentalism of the South welcomed the Jew with cordiality.

But there was more to it than Protestant Fundamentalism. The Jew was nearly always self-employed. Far into the late 1960's the Jews of the South, except for a few professionals—doctors, lawyers, and teachers—represented a single proprietary class, which gave them immediate identity with those people in the community who have since become known as the power structure.

The social segregation between Jew and Gentile has always remained rigid, but between 9 A.M. and 5 P.M., five days a week, the Jew's business status gave him an identity with the most influential citizens of his town or city, the banker, the real estate broker, the fuel oil distributor, the lawyer, the contractor, the trucker, the power company, and the Chamber of Commerce. In the main the Jews of the South strengthened this 9 A.M. to 5 P.M. alliance by reflecting the habits, attitudes, politics, and often the prejudices of the Establishment.

But it was precisely the Jew's identity with the power structure that worked against him whenever demagogic orators held forth against Wall Street or "international bankers." "Our Negro brethren, too, are being held in bondage by Rothschild," said North Carolina's Elias Carr in nearly every speech. Carr became governor of North

Carolina (1893–97) as a Democrat who could presumably silence populistic opponents of the state's political Establishment by employing, at least, their rhetorical anti-Semitism.

A famous itinerant evangelist, Mordecai Ham, pitched his tent sermons on the theme of Jewish wealth and capitalism. But old Mordecai lived long enough to inveigh against Jews, in another generation, for conspiring to destroy free enterprise.

Unlike the power structure in metropolitan centers of the North, the Southerner saw no Jewish garment workers, garbage collectors, street cleaners, policemen, janitors, clerks, truck drivers and taxi drivers, and furthermore, in the absence of the Jewish slum or ghetto of the Northern city, a demagogue such as Tom Watson could easily make the poor of the South believe that "The Jews have all the money."

In the civil rights movements, 1954–1965, the local Jewish communities of the South took a more or less active part, *only* after the power structure of their city finally said the time had come—as in Charlotte, Richmond, Atlanta, and most of the other cities in the upper South, of 50,000 population and over—but where the surrounding society has remained rigid, as in Mississippi and Alabama, the Jewish communities have remained silent, except for two or three embattled rabbis. Since the beginning of the black civil rights movement, the Southerner has feared the black, the Jew has feared the Southerner, and the black has feared no one.

One of the points I am at pains to convey to Jewish readers is that during this black revolution they are getting a free ride. Usually I make this point when I am asked about black anti-Semitism. A black anti-Semite, I explain, is about as convincing as a Jewish white supremacist. The two luxuries of Western civilization, anti-Semitism and Negrophobia, are denied us. But we have had some advantages, the chief of which is that the struggle of the NAACP and Martin Luther King and Jim Farmer to advance black equality has made the Constitution of the United States a living document. This struggle has convinced Americans, and continues to convince them every day, that the Constitution means just what it says. This is no mean accomplishment in industrialized twentieth-century America. It has strengthened my security and the security of my grandchildren.

Two Sides of the Coin

THE JEWS have always been concerned about two forces that have threatened to destroy them as an ethnic group. One of these is anti-Semitism, and the other is assimilation into the surrounding culture. In Europe both of these threats have almost always been accompanied by the fortunes or misfortunes of the culture which happens at the time to be host to the Jewish community. Persecution of the Jews, emancipation, or assimilation of the Jews runs concurrent with prosperity, hardship, or some sort of national crisis. In America, however, the fate of the Jews has had no such intimate connection with the condition of the nation as a whole.

Consider the case of black emancipation and what it meant to the political and social history of the United States, and you will understand the difference between the

Jews, whose status in this country was never really a matter of debate or controversy, and the status of a group whose position was hotly contested, almost from the very beginning up until the present time. In France, Germany, Russia, and Poland, the status of the Jews was almost always considered an area in need of reform or readjustment, especially during periods of revolution. Such a consideration, furthermore, was only the beginning of a great many long stories in European history, for if the status of the Jews was an issue raised by one or another revolution, so reactions and counterreactions became a social pattern after the revolution and more or less guaranteed the continuation of anti-Semitic periods in subsequent history.

The Jews of America suffered no such consideration or ups and downs to their residency here. The American Revolution did not divide the nation into opposing groups, for it was directed in essence against outsiders, and at the time the status of the American Jewish community was simply not a part of the overall national concern. In a way the same relationship applied in the British revolution led by Cromwell: The "Jewish question" was not an intrinsic part of the revolutionary program. And though increased numbers of Jews entered the British community, there was never any positive identification an anti-Semite or even a pro-Semite might make as regards overall revolutionary aims.

American anti-Semitism and British anti-Semitism, for that matter, have much in common and probably for the reasons already stated: In neither country was the Jewish problem any more than incidental or peripheral to the general aims or destiny of the nation as a whole. In both countries anti-Semitism has been practiced by insignificant, powerless groups or individuals considered marginal by the total society. We refer, of necessity, to Britain after the Tudors.

By way of contrast, anti-Semitic movements in France, Germany, Poland, and Russia have usually occupied a prominent position in the national politics of those countries, and the groups or individuals involved have frequently exercised great political power—in some cases gained chiefly by virtue of the anti-Semitism itself! In effect, an ambitious Frenchman, Pole, German, or Russian could rise to power by making it known he hated the Jews.

Although this phenomenon is not altogether unknown in America, generally the pattern of anti-Semitism is a different matter, something that occurs throughout the Diaspora regardless of political positions or aims. It might be termed casual anti-Semitism or the anti-Semitism of emotional impulse.

A Pattern of Philo Semitism

THUS THE SOUTHERN LANDSMAN, which brings us to the very beginnings of what made the Jewish communities of the South.

Despite the pinpricks of anti-Semitism: exclusion from the country clubs, the city clubs, the Mardi Gras, etc. Nevertheless the preponderant Gentile section of America offers an unusual opportunity to study the "ingredients" which have coalesced into the completely free society, and which in specific terms of the South may rightfully be called a 300-year-old pattern of American philo Semitism.

What then are these ingredients? One point in particular

impresses itself immediately. The new eighteenth-century attitude toward the Jews was not an American innovation, but a common development of the Anglo-Saxon world. It was not geography that ameliorated the savage prejudices of the Old World, but an idea—a humanism which had its roots in the Anglo-Calvinist-Dutch Reformed tradition of the British Isles and Holland. When the Dutch lost Brazil to Portugal, the Jews again had to seek out Dutch or Anglo-Saxons, and that was the year 1654. It was specifically this Atlantic-Puritan nexus which produced a Roger Williams in New England, a William Penn in Pennsylvania, and a John Locke in the Carolinas. They gave expression to this new idea, of which the philosopher Rabbi Leo Baeck has said: "It broke all ties with antiquity . . . it no longer carried the Middle Ages on its back." Immediately in the wake of the French Huguenots, Germans, Moravians, Quakers, and Jews, this Anglo-Saxon society in the South invited the philosopher John Locke to lay the foundation for a new tradition in terms of this idea. In the same year (1668) that the Ukrainian Bogdan Chmielnicki was massacring more than a half million Jews in Eastern Europe, Locke wrote the Fundamental Constitutions for the South: ". . . in as ample manner as they [the people] might desire, freedom and liberty of conscience in all religious or spiritual things." The Constitution expressly stated that as "Jews, heathens, and other dissenters" might be induced to settle in the colony, "any seven or more persons agreeing in any religion shall constitute a church or profession."

In the same year (1776) that the "liberal" Frederick the Great restricted the number of Jewish marriages to a minimum per annum (and then only on condition that the couple would buy $300 worth of chinaware from his royal

porcelain factory), Thomas Jefferson and America embla-
zoned the sky with the declaration that "all men are
created equal, that they are endowed by their Creator with
the unalienable right to life, liberty and the pursuit of
happiness."

These Anglo-Saxons who left their country and faced the
dangers of the ocean to seek in the wilderness of North
America the right to worship God according to the dictates
of their own conscience had created a new idea in human
relations. And for the first time in the history of the
Dispersion, the Jews did not enter a new land under
sufferance or even by "negotiation." The Anglo-Saxons had
eliminated the "host" and "guest" relationship. The immigrant of today was by right the "host" of tomorrow. But so
far-reaching an advance in intellectual humanism could
not come overnight. The precursors of this Americanism
did not quite know from the beginning how to solve the
problem of the relation of their faiths to this new idea. The
Anglican Church attempted to establish the pattern merely
by weight of numbers. In North Carolina this tradition
persisted, at least on paper, for nearly a century after the
establishment of the Bill of Rights. A constitutional provision forbade public office to anyone who denied the "being
of God or the truth of the Protestant religion, or the divine
authority of either the Old or the New Testament or who
shall hold religious principles incompatible with the freedom and safety of the State." It is pertinent to our study to
note carefully that during the entire ninety-year debate for
the repeal of this provision, I have been unable to uncover a
single derogatory reference to the Jews as a people. The
provision involved Catholics, Jews, Quakers, and Deists
and was clearly in conflict with Article IX of the Bill of
Rights. But there was no pride in this constitutional

provision, and, as a matter of fact, Catholics, Jews, Quakers, and Deists had held public office. An effort to expel Jacob Henry, a Jew, had failed in 1809. Jacob Henry had been elected to the state legislature in 1808. A year later, upon reflection, an opponent tried to unseat him and based his action upon the provision in the state constitution which required "belief in the divine authority of the New Testament."

Let us turn our attention to England again. The Catholics were admitted to the British House of Commons in 1828, the Jews in 1858, and the rationalists, who refused to take an oath in the name of any God, in 1884. It was no coincidence that North Carolina followed in almost perfect chronological order.

In South Carolina we find that an anomalous condition arose. The state constitution established by the Provincial Congress contained no religious liberty provision. Neither did it provide for any religious test. The Episcopalians had been given legal status, and while the church made no attempt to interfere with the religious freedom of other sects, there was always a chance that a liberal atmosphere could change. Legislation is the key to our American freedom. Put it on the books. Nothing is as important as that. A Presbyterian clergyman, the Reverend William Tennent, saw the danger. He called for law—a statute specifically guaranteeing religious freedom. In the session of 1778 his efforts were rewarded. He won the support of three political stalwarts, General Christopher Gadsden, Charles Pinckney, and Rawlins Lowndes. In 1790 a new constitution was adopted which granted full religious rights to all, including all civil privileges to Catholics, Jews, and freethinkers. South Carolina went further even than Virginia. In its constitution granting religious and civil freedom, the South Carolinians, after listing a few of the minority sects, added the phrase "and all of mankind." Charles Pinckney was the man. Quite a man. He was chairman of the 1790 convention and the principal agent in removing forever all civil and political disabilities that had been imposed on Jews and other minorities in South Carolina. Mr. Pinckney was obsessed with the ideas of religious and political freedom. Remember that he was a delegate to the Federal Constitutional Convention in 1787. He kept hammering away at the idea of religious and political freedom. He proposed: "The legislature of the United States shall pass no law on the subject of religion." That did not satisfy him entirely. Again he sent up a proposal: "No religious test or qualification shall ever be annexed to any office under the United States." They were discussing the oath of office. Pinckney thought about that for a while. He proposed that after the word "oath" the phrase "or affirmation" be added. Pinckney was thinking of Quakers and others who may not wholly subscribe to the idea of taking an oath. He wanted a clause in the Constitution to read: "No religious test shall ever be required as a qualification to any office or public trust under the authority of the United States." Mr. Pinckney had another suggestion. He wanted the United States to establish a national university. Mr. James Madison associated himself with Mr. Pinckney on this idea—and again in his university proposal Mr. Pinckney left nothing to chance: ". . . to establish a university in which no preference of distinction should be allowed on account of religion." Gouverneur Morris objected to the university idea. Mr. Morris' contention was that the "central government" already had the power to establish a university if it saw fit to do so, and therefore the motion was unnecessary.

232

The proposal was defeated with South Carolina, Virginia, and Pennsylvania voting in the affirmative. Mr. Pinckney was a philosopher. He could see all too well that the minds of men, and of nations, are not wholly excellent or uninterruptedly independent. Therefore he hoped that when arrogance and fear or some other self-deceiving emotion plays upon us, we will be well fortified to withstand the threat.

When I think of Charles Pinckney of South Carolina, I recall what Clarence Darrow once said: "There is always one man." There was always *one* man in every age, in every country, in every benighted corner of the world, in every dark era of our history, one man who stood up and said: "This far and no farther," one man was always there who fought for human dignity. Because of Pinckney and others like him, Bernard M. Baruch's portrait hangs in the State Capitol at Columbia.

The General Gadsden of this fight for religious freedom in South Carolina had learned Hebrew from his Jewish fellow captives during his long imprisonment by the British in the American Revolution. He made a handsome present to the Beth Elohim Congregation at Charleston. He presented them with the Mishnah and the works of Maimonides in Hebrew. Nearly a half century earlier, John Wesley, founder of the Church of Methodism, studied Spanish in order to converse with the Jews of Savannah, Georgia. And 100 years earlier, in 1655, Harvard College established a chair in Hebrew under Judah Monis "for the education of the English and Indian youth in knowledge and godliness."

In the constitutional process of the free society, religious freedom is the last to be developed and to become perfect, as demonstrated by the example of England and America, as well as after the French Revolution. The memories of common persecutions, however, were finally the cause, through necessary evolution, of the glorious and full emancipation of religion, taught to the world by the English-speaking civilization.

When we discuss the Jewish people of the South, we are on solid ground when we look at them as a continuing culture and tradition. This is true not only of the Jew, but of all our peoples. Certainly the mind and the heart of two sections of North Carolina reflect more than the physical presence of Moravians and Waldensians but go back to their roots in the forests of Bohemia and the Po Valley. And what we call the American way of life within our Carolina society is anchored deeply in the traditions and cultures of the British Isles. Thus, it is proper that we approach the history of the Jewish people, as a people, as a continuing cultural and religious group, and on that basis our findings dwarf the combined influence of all the individuals within the group over these entire 300 years. This influence is clearly stamped upon the consciousness of North Carolina and South Carolina, as indeed it is stamped upon the whole of the Christian civilization. You have but to travel a few miles in any direction to come under its influence: Pisgah, Cedars of Lebanon, Mount Olive, Mount Gilead, Mount Hebron, Nebo, Ararat, Winston-Salem, and at every cross-roads, the inscription: "This way to Beth El Chapel." And Jacob called the place Beth El. House of God. And from the pulpit of every church of every denomination, the Hebraic ideal:

It hath been told thee, O Man, what is good,
And what the Lord doth require of thee;
Only to do justice, and to love mercy, and
to walk humbly, with thy God.

234

In this interpretation of our history the life of the Jewish people within this society takes on its proper perspective: the substance which it has in truth transferred to the ebb and flow of the daily life of the Gentile community in which it has lived in peace and prosperity.

It has further historical significance. In fact it assumes great proportions in keeping with the history of America as a nation; the story of the transplanting of the Nordic, Mediterranean, and African cultures which compose the fabric of this country. Look at it once, a few scattered settlements along the Atlantic seaboard. Look at it again, a mighty nation—the mightiest nation the world has ever seen. Where did they come from? Clerks and soldiers from England, seamen from Scotland, laborers from Ireland, miners from Wales, woodcutters from Sweden, farmers from Italy and Germany, tailors from Russia, blacks from Africa; Christian and Jew, the pious and the unchurched, the disinherited and the adventurers, the persecuted, the tired and the homeless; and they became Americans—Americans all. Woodrow Wilson was right—America is nothing except in terms of every one of them.

America Is Different
(An Aside)

THE JEWISH COMPONENT in the population of the United States dates its true beginnings from a point in history which to many European Jewish communities came only after centuries of struggle and adjustment. This point is of course the emancipation of the Jews, which came relatively late to the Jewish settlements in the Old World,

235

but which was more or less a given circumstance of American Jewry.

The Jews of France, Germany, and Russia had struggled to establish themselves as a free people, and the struggle blended into the period of emancipation and inevitably colored it, made it continuous with Jewish culture and feeling, and indeed, Jewish existence.

The true history of the Jews in America begins after the emancipation.

American Jews never became involved in the "dream" of European Jewry, that all the problems would evaporate with the advent of freedom. The Zionist movement, which came about as a reaction to the idea of emancipation, and the concept of diaspora nationalism existed in America only as reflected, half-hearted "causes." If they ever got off the ground at all, they did so without the intensity and the passion of their European counterparts.

We do have a group in America, it is true, which calls itself the American Council for Judaism and which pursues emancipation with some vigor. But it is an organization that in the absence of any opposition lacks true vitality. For no one in America makes an issue of emancipation, since it has been one of the accepted features of American Jewry almost from the beginning. At the same time, even the American Council recognizes the futility of the position of earlier Old World Jewish groups that emancipation represents a solution to Jewish problems.

Given the peculiar nature of the Jews' participation in American history, the issue might accurately be stated, as in fact Abraham Cahan stated it some eighty years ago, that the only Jewish problem in America is how to prevent the emergence of a Jewish problem.

Epilogue

AND THUS THE JEWS of the South, an episodic history of ebbs and surges. The Civil War, the emergence of the Ku Klux Klan, the industrialization and urbanization of the South directly affected Jews.

But cross burning or the failure of the cotton crop never affected the core of the American Jewish community because the core of that community was never in the South.

The residency of Jews in North America has been marked by their gathering in the cities. Of the 6,200,000 Jews in the United States today, 4,000,000 live in sixteen major cities, only two of which are remotely Southern— Baltimore and Miami, and they contain only 200,000 Jews.

Labor agitation in Northern cities, beginning with the turn of the century, affected American Jews far more than anything which transpired in the South. Jews in the North transformed some unions into Jewish unions.

There were Jews in the South before there was a South. Forty-two Jews, we have seen, landed in Savannah six months after Oglethorpe established the crown colony of Georgia in 1733. But the march of the Spaniards up from St. Augustine with their attendant Inquisition frightened all but two Jewish families away in 1742.

Many Jews left the South after the Civil War. Anti-Semitism, engendered by the passion of secession, sent the Strauses, the Lehmans, the Baruchs, and hundreds of other Jews north where they became the "Our Crowd" of the post-Civil War era.

Another wave of anti-Semitism, this one fed by the cruel industrialization of 1900 capitalistic mores, sent the Jews of Georgia packing. And the Jews in New York hesitated to start out in North Carolina or Tennessee.

One of the truths about the South is that it does not have a continuous history for any of its people. The Civil War broke the South in two, and the South is still contending with the twentieth century over what kind of place it should be. Black history in the South is now at a standstill. It started with slavery, felt elevation with Reconstruction, was punished by Jim Crowism, came alive again with the civil rights movement, culminating with the March on Washington in 1963, the high-water mark of liberalism, and now the history is stalled, blacks and racists and the indifferent waiting to see what will happen.

The South undergoes the historical process convulsively. Convulsions are one of the things Jews don't need.

To survive the convulsions, the Jews in the South were part of the landscape. They were secessionists when Sumter was fired upon and gradualists when the White Citizens Councils proliferated.

What now distinguishes the Jews among the other minorities in the South is the realization that they are all in the same boat. The Holocaust has convinced them there are no special privileges for anyone. All of them are Zionists, champions of Israel, but they seem to have little other political coloration.

In the North, and in California and in Chicago, Jews have a political identity. The question of whether Jews would vote for Nixon or McGovern was an interesting, if foregone, speculation in the election of 1972. But it did not interest Southerners, first, because there were not enough Jews to make a difference and, second, because there was no squabbling among the Jews there to make people wonder. Jews below the Mason-Dixon Line ceded the political initiative years ago.

Southerners don't worry about Jews because Jews do not threaten them socially. For many years the Jews were a single proprietary class. They sold ready-to-wear clothing for women or they ran jewelry stores or they shipped peaches, but they were never employees angling for the vice-presidency of the corporation.

Jewish contact with the Gentiles is through the power structure with the banker who lends the money for capital investment, with the lawyer who draws up the contract, with the realtor who rents property, and with the income tax expert. No hotel ever boasts of a restricted clientele because there are simply not enough Jews to go around.

Jewish identity in the South is based more on religion than ethnicity. Some schoolboys in Charlotte now wear yarmulkes to school. Elsewhere schoolboys also wear yarmulkes, but elsewhere schoolboys *always* wore yarmulkes.

When I first arrived in Charlotte in the early 1940's, there wasn't a delicatessen between Miami and Washington, D.C. Now Charlotte has not only a venerable delicatessen, but two kosher butcher shops. There were probably 3,000 Jews in North Carolina in 1942. There are some 8,000 today congregated in Raleigh, Greensboro, and Charlotte.

The lone Jew in a Southern town is now an anachronism. Jewish shopkeepers since the 1950's have been moving to the large cities, following the pioneering malls which attract buyers from whole areas rather than discreet points.

In St. Matthews, South Carolina, the "Jew store" has long been run by a Christian, a graduate of the Textile Division of North Carolina State College. He operates the establishment for an absentee owner, who putters around a golf course in one of those automatic carts with a gay umbrella.

Acknowledgments

I ACKNOWLEDGE with gratitude the use of the following books in the preparation of this work:

Coit, Margaret L., *Mr. Baruch.* Boston, Houghton Mifflin, 1957.

Fast, Howard, *Jews.* New York, Dial Press, 1969.

Golden, Harry, and Rywell, Martin, *Jews in American History.*

Gunther, John, *Inside U.S.A.* New York, Harper & Bros., 1951.

Korn, Berton W., *The Early Jews of New Orleans.* New York, American Jewish Historical Society, 1969.

Pollock, Barbara, *The Collectors—Dr. Claribel and Miss Etta Cone.* Indianapolis, Bobbs-Merrill.

Rothschild, Janice O., *"As But a Day," The First 100 Years of the Temple, Atlanta, Georgia.* Atlanta, Hebrew Benevolent Congregation.

Simonhoff, Harry, *Jewish Participants in the Civil War.* New York, Arco.

———, *Saga of American Jewry.* New York, Arco, 1959.

Sklare, Marshall, ed., *The Jews: Social Patterns of an American Group.* Glencoe, Ill., Free Press, 1958.

Weisbord, Robert G., and Stein, Arthur, *A Bittersweet Encounter: The Afro-American and the American Jew.* New York, Schocken, 1972.

In addition, I received some valuable assistance from Rabbi Jack Segal of the Congregation Beth Yeshurun, Houston, Texas; Rabbi Edward L. Cohn, Kahali Kadosh Beth Elohim, Charleston, South Carolina; Rabbi Sidney Lefkowitz, Temple Ahasath Chesed of Jacksonville, Florida; and Adolph Rosenberg, editor of *The Southern Israelite*, Atlanta, Georgia.

Index

Goldstein, Mrs. Maurice W., 205
Gompers, Samuel, 149
Goodfriend, Isaac, 79
Goodman, Arthur, 174
Goodman, David, 205
Graham, Frank P., 180
Grant, Samuel, 51
Grant, Ulysses S., 121, 141
Gratz, Bernard, 62–63
Gray Fox (Davis), 27
Grayson, Cary T., 149
Greenblatt, Robert, 70
Greenfield, Jack, 92
Greenhow, Rose, 115–16
Greensboro, North Carolina, Jews of, 21, 163–65, 239
Griffin, Marvin, 74
Grynspan, Diego, 96
Gutheim, James, 114–15

Haas, Caroline, 69
Haas, Jacob, 68–69
Hagerstown *Mail*, 64
Ham, Mordecai, 225
Handlin, Oscar, 22, 161
Hanna, Mark, 132
Harby, Isaac, 218–19
Harby, Leonara De Lyon, 220
Harby, Levi Charles, 219
Harby, Levi Myers, 219–20
Harrison, Benjamin, 30–31, 103
Harrison, William Henry, 103
Har Sinai Congregation, Baltimore, 110
Hart, Jacob, 186
Hart, Philip, 42
Hartsfield, William B., 71, 74
Harvard College, 233
Hawkins, Colonel, 28
Hays, Moses Michael, 182
Hebrew Academy, Atlanta, 72

Hebrew Benevolent Association, Camden, N.C., 144
Hebrew Benevolent Congregation, Atlanta, 75
Hebrew Benevolent Society, Charlotte, 178–79
Hebrew Cemetery, Charlotte, 175, 177–79
Hebrew College, 31
Hebrew Union College, 100
Hecht, Robert, 209
Heine, Heinrich, 192
Hellman, Isaiah Wolf, 21–22
Henrietta Maria, Queen, 60
Henriques, Isaac Nunes, 39
Henry, Jacob, 55, 174, 231
Herman, David, 189
Heustis, James F., 127
Heustis, Rachel Lyons, 127
Hirsch, Bennett, 205
Hirshinger, Jay, 175, 178
Hitler, Adolf, 90, 95, 101, 151
Holmes, Oliver Wendell, Jr., 85–86
Horvitz, Leo, 210
Houston, Texas, Jews of, 207–13
Houston University, 210
Howard, Oliver Otis, 222
Howe, Louis, 150
Howe, Robert, 43
Hughes, Charles Evans, 85

Ichay, Robert, 80
Immigrant Jews, 20–21, 22, 29–31, 35, 38–40, 63, 65, 96, 111, 158, 188, 193, 194, 215, 224, 235
Intermarriage, 98–100, 127, 186–87, 189, 190–92, 206, 210–11
International Ladies Garment Workers Union, 22, 193
Isaacs, Isaiah, 31–32, 49, 50–51
Israel, Michael, 55–56

Temple Congregation, Atlanta, 79
Temple Emanu-El, New York City, 114
Temple Israel Congregation, Charlotte, 174, 175
Temple Sinai Congregation, Atlanta, 80
Tennent, William, 231
Texas, Jews of, 206–13
Texas University, 206
Thomas, Ebenezer, 65, 66
Titanic, RMS, 198
Tocqueville, Alexis de, 68, 104–5
Toms, Rosalind, 64
Tondee, Peter, 41
Touro, Isaac, 182
Touro, Judah, 182–85
Touro, Reyna Hays, 182
Towerculla, Chief, 28–29
Trachtenberg, Dr., 182
Trinity College, North Carolina, 222
Truman, Harry S., 153–54, 155
Tugwell, Rexford G., 150
Twiggs, David Emanuel, 118, 127
Tyler, John, 184

Union Society, 41, 54–55
Union Theological Seminary, Cincinnati, 21
United Daughters of the Confederacy, 132, 133, 145
United Jewish Appeal, 73, 97, 175, 182, 187, 208, 217

Van Straaton, H., 178
Vance, Zebulon, 129
Virginia, Jews of, 24–25, 31, 32, 46–53, 59–60, 89–90; American Revolution and, 55–56
Virginia Constitution, 56

Wade, Benjamin Franklin, 131
Walker, James J., 200
War of 1812, 29, 56, 183, 185–86, 217, 219
War with Amalek (Einhorn), 111–12
Warrington, North Carolina, Jews of, 220
Washington, D.C., Jews of, 64
Washington, George, 25, 30, 55, 56
Watson, Tom, 83–84, 86, 88, 225
Watson's Jeffersonian Magazine, 83
Webster, Daniel, 184
Wecker, Der, 112
Weekly Jeffersonian, 83
Weil, Gertrude, 180–81
Weil, Henry, 179, 180
Weil, Herman, 179
Weil, Mina Rosenthal, 180
Weil, Solomon, 179
Weill, Will, 178
Weiner, Sol, 209
Weingarten, Bernard, 209
Weinstein, John, 187
Weinstein, Milton, 70
Wesley, John, 233
Western Reserve, 19
Westwood Country Club, Houston, 207
Whisper My Name (Davis), 26, 27
Whitaker, J. B., 179
White, Harvey, 136
Whitlock, Elizabeth, 32, 49–50
Whitney, Eli, 103
Willard, Daniel, 148
William of Orange, 61
Williamsburg, Virginia, Jews of, 24, 46
Williamson, Major, 58
Wilson, Woodrow, 148, 149, 235
Wise, Stephen, 90
Witten, Mrs. Paul J., 205

Wolff, Albert, 171
Wolfson, Mrs. Beryl, 189
World War I, 199
World War II, 151, 152
Wyatt, Henry, 135
Wyeth, John A., 145

Yanceyville, North Carolina, Jews of,
32–33
Yeshiva High School, Atlanta, 72
Yulee, David Levi, 126, 214

Zionism, 236